RANDOM TANGENTS:

Embracing Adventures in Life

GREG HAWK

DESERT ROAMER PRESS
Cheyenne, Wyoming

Random Tangents: Embracing Adventures in Life
© 2020, Greg Hawk. All rights reserved.

ISBN 978-1-7344884-0-1 (paperback)
ISBN 978-1-7344884-1-8(eBook)
Library of Congress Control Number: 2020906018

www.desertroamerpress.com

Without limiting the rights under copyright reserved above, no part of this publication may be reproduced, stored in or introduced into a retrieval system, or transmitted in any form or by any means (electronic, mechanical, photocopying, recording or otherwise whether now or hereafter known), without the prior written permission of both the copyright owner and the above publisher of this book, except by a reviewer who wishes to quote brief passages in connection with a review written for insertion in a magazine, newspaper, broadcast, website, blog or other outlet in conformity with United States and International Fair Use or comparable guidelines to such copyright exceptions.

This book is intended to provide accurate information with regard to its subject matter and reflects the opinion and perspective of the author. However, in times of rapid change, ensuring all information provided is entirely accurate and up-to-date at all times is not always possible. Therefore, the author and publisher accept no responsibility for inaccuracies or omissions and specifically disclaim any liability, loss or risk, personal, professional or otherwise, which may be incurred as a consequence, directly or indirectly, of the use and/or application of any of the contents of this book.

Disclaimer:

This book is a memoir by the author and some names of the people involved have been changed to protect their identities. There are no fictional characters in this book.

The last chapters in this book are on the author and his treasure hunting escapades and should be read as entertainment. If you decide to look for any of these treasures please research the ownership of the property and laws pertaining to said property.

I wish to dedicate this book to all the people whom I have had the pleasure or displeasure of meeting in my lifetime. Each one had an impact, whether it was a word, a sentence, or an emotion, either as a friend or an antagonist. One never knows the conscious and unconscious effects any one of these interactions can have on you as you chart your course through life. I am happy where I am now, so thanks to all!

A special dedication to my two children for loving, understanding, and putting up with their eccentric father.

ARE YOU CHASING LIFE OR
IS LIFE CHASING YOU?
THAT IS THE QUESTION!

Contents

1 Gypsy 1
2 Small-Town Boy 4
3 Army Days 7
4 Quan Loi 13
5 Homeward Bound 33
6 The American Dream 40
7 Cutting Loose: Truk Lagoon 52
8 Adventure Bound: New Zealand 78
9 Into the Fire 86
10 Starting Over: Australia 90
11 Aqua Time Venture: Hong Kong 125
12 The Hunt Begins 139
13 Lost Dutchman Mine 150
14 Heart Mountain 165
15 Lost Confederate Gold 176
16 Lost Meteorite 187
17 Treasure on the Colorado 197
18 The Lost Ivanpah Silver Vein 205
19 End of the Hunt 213
    Epilogue 221
    About the Author 225

CHAPTER ONE
Gypsy

It was March of 1984. I had just touched down in Auckland, New Zealand, and made my way to the Sheraton, where I had a room reserved. A beautiful young lady, Molly, who was checking me in, just happened to be single. We went out to dinner that evening and I ended up spending all my time with her over the next two weeks.

The first week we stayed at her apartment and I worked on helping her fix it up as she had just moved in. Auckland was quaint, with milk delivery to your doorstep and the meat shop down the street next to the veggie shop. At that time there were no large grocery store chains in the city. There wasn't central heat or air conditioning in the old house she lived in, either. For heat you plugged in the electric heaters and to cool things a bit you turned on the fans and opened the windows. Temperatures in Auckland were mild year-round.

Molly was taking some acting classes and had dreams of becoming an actress; I encouraged her. She looked somewhat like Marilyn Monroe with blond hair and an innocence that drew me to her. Everyone must have a dream and give it 100 percent, and if it doesn't materialize, at least you won't have to say, "If only I had tried harder."

We talked about astrology and different facets of the New Age era that I had been delving into. Seeing my interest, she

RANDOM TANGENTS

said she knew of a gypsy lady from Romania who read tarot cards and asked if I wanted to go to see her. My first thought was, "Here I am, a macho guy, going to see a fortune teller. Right." Then I thought, "Why not? It will be a totally different experience in life."

Molly made an appointment for me and drove me to a small white house where the gypsy lady lived. She said she would wait in the car, so I walked up to the house and knocked on the front door. A short, heavy-set lady with deep brown eyes answered the door, showed me into her living room, and motioned for me to sit down at the table. She sat across from me and handed me a big deck of worn-out tarot cards and told me to shuffle them. She said that she could sense that I had a very strong mind and was a forward thinker. She was chatty and said a lot of other things during the reading. The main things I remember her mentioning were:

- "A green-eyed girl from Los Angeles will appear again in your life."
- "Beware of a vehicle that looks like a station wagon."
- "I see a two-story white house overlooking the ocean."
- "I see a woman with two rings, and she has a child."
- "You will have a neck injury in or around water."
- "You will have a lower leg injury around snow."
- "You will not spend your last days in the United States."

When she mentioned a green-eyed girl from Los Angeles (LA), I thought it was all BS as I didn't know any girl from LA. But when the reading was over and I was making my way back to the car, the green-eyed girl suddenly made sense. I had met her in Tahiti four months ago at the hotel on Moorea!

GYPSY

Before I left, the gypsy woman gave me her phone number and said that if I ever wanted to contact her and ask a question, I could—we had a connection. I didn't keep the phone number, but looking back, I probably should have.

As this story unfolds, five of the gypsy's predictions were revealed to be glaringly accurate. They didn't happen the way I had visualized them, but they came true nonetheless. Life has yet to reveal the other two. My life to this point was a series of events that often ran up against a wall forcing me to take another direction or tangent in the course of life.

CHAPTER TWO
Small-Town Boy

Growing up in the small farm town of Dalton City, Illinois, set the foundation for my future. During the summer, I worked for farmers baling hay and cutting weeds out of soybeans to make a little money for school clothes. When I got to be fifteen years old, I worked in construction with my father, learning different trades and how to run heavy equipment (which I disliked).

After high school I went to college at Southern Illinois University in Carbondale, Illinois, from 1966 to 1968. Even though I took interest in the design department, I didn't know what I wanted to be or do and felt that I was wasting money and time. Hell, I still don't know what I want to do!

In the spring of 1967, while still in college, a friend of mine and I decided to go down to Ft. Lauderdale, Florida, for spring break. I had an uncle who lived down there that we could stay with, so it wasn't going to cost much except for fuel. We started driving from Illinois and stopped in Kentucky for dinner. We were filling up and asked the old boy at the gas station if he knew of a good restaurant close by. When giving us directions to the restaurant, he advised us to tell them Mel sent us and they would serve us something to drink, as legally it was a dry county.

SMALL-TOWN BOY

We went to the restaurant and, yes, they were selling bootleg whiskey, which we didn't need as we were planning on driving all night. The food was good, but the entertainment was even better. There were two guys and a gal sitting in the next booth, telling stories while they were choking down a few beers, and we started listening. With their southern accents and storytelling abilities, their conversation kept us laughing afterwards just remembering the punch lines.

We finished dinner and headed down the road. It was my turn to drive while my friend took a nap. As time went on, I got drowsy, drifted off the road, and sideswiped a bridge abutment. The damage down the side of my car was nothing compared to what it could have been. If we had hit the abutment head on, I wouldn't be here today. It was a wake-up call to how fragile life is and a foreshadowing that I can reflect back on. Death can come quickly and at any time! I made sure to get the damage fixed once we arrived in Ft. Lauderdale as I didn't want my father to know about it once I returned home.

In the summer of 1968, I left college and started running heavy equipment for my father, excavating basements and crawl spaces for houses around Decatur, Illinois. My father spent twenty-two years working as a foreman at a soybean plant in Decatur before being injured on the job. His back was broken, and it took two years and two operations to get him back together so he could walk. During those two years our family had no income as the company doctor said there was nothing wrong with him, so he was not entitled to any compensation. He had to hire a lawyer, who helped him receive a settlement of $60,000 after the surgeries. Of course, a third of that went to the lawyer. After the settlement, my father was told by the

RANDOM TANGENTS

company he had worked for that they no longer had a position for him. He had been loyal to the company, wasn't in the union, and years later when he turned sixty-five, he got a measly $50 per month retirement check. Peanuts for twenty-two years of his life!

After he was let go, he was trying to make it as a contractor even though his back was never the same. Before he got hurt, my father was six feet tall and weighed 240 pounds—all muscle. He would pick my one hundred-pound body up with one hand and laugh. After the surgeries, he could lay block and brick but couldn't bend over far.

He was hardheaded, and I seemed to mirror this quality. One day, when he didn't like the way I was digging a basement for a new house, I turned off the equipment, crawled out of the hole, and told him that I quit. We probably should have talked things out, but that wasn't the way of things back then. People were raised to be tough. You kept your emotions to yourself without expressing them, and when things went too far, you just changed course and took off on another tangent. I knew my parents loved me, but not once did I ever hear my father say it. When he was in his eighties, I told him I loved him, and he broke down crying.

Now what? I had my fill of running equipment. Should I wait to get drafted and sent to Vietnam, or go and join up? I decided to sign up to become a helicopter pilot. I thought it would be cool to become a pilot. How little did I know. My father wasn't happy about me joining as he had served for seven years in the Army before and during World War II. I had ninety days before I had to appear at the induction headquarters, so I painted our house for my mother before leaving. My father and I didn't talk much that summer.

CHAPTER THREE
Army Days

It was October of 1968 when I was inducted into the Army at St. Louis, Missouri, and was then sent to Ft. Polk, Louisiana, for basic training. We arrived in the middle of the night and they fed us something I couldn't identify; I thought it was squirrel or raccoon. It certainly wasn't a vacation resort.

The first day there, I got my eyes tested for flight training as a prerequisite for helicopter school. The tests came back, and it seemed that one of my eyes wouldn't focus fast enough. That put a quick end to my helicopter career. However, I had already signed an agreement with the Army saying that if I didn't pass my flight physical, I would automatically become a two-year enlisted man with a choice of military occupational specialty (MOS). I looked through a catalog of different job descriptions and chose to be an airport controller. Soon, I learned that in the Army you do not always get what you signed up for.

While at Ft. Polk I noticed that a lot of the soldiers stationed there were recently back from Vietnam. Many of them had patches on their shoulders showing that they had been attached to the 1st Cavalry Division or the 1st Infantry Division. It was obvious that these two divisions were probably catching a lot of hell over there as many of the returning soldiers had been wounded.

RANDOM TANGENTS

Ft. Polk was known for its "tiger land," which was built for advanced infantry training for soldiers going over to Vietnam. It was hot and humid as hell during the summer, which gave one the taste of what it was going to be like over there. Luckily, I was there during the winter season. We learned how to march, dress, become proficient with our M14 rifles, and take orders. There was plenty of physical training to get us in top shape, which was supported by a lean diet. We were divided into squads in our barracks and learned how to work and live together.

While there, our squad was ordered to go on a burial detail. This was not the first time I had attended a funeral. When I was four years old, my aunt and uncle were hit by a carload of drunks while driving across a bridge, and she was instantly killed. Death produced such a definite void for ones that were still living. Later, when I was twelve, my grandmother died, which also caused great grief for the family. I will always remember the silver casket and the smell of all the flowers. That is probably why I have never bought a silver car or liked flowers all that much. These were my first experiences with death. Now I was getting a whole different perspective.

We practiced the whole funeral drill several times to make sure we were proficient in our actions at the service. The next day we boarded a bus to a small-town cemetery in Louisiana where the service was going to be held. Our drill sergeant and first lieutenant accompanied us as representatives for the Army. We performed the service with a three-volley rifle salute, which represents duty, honor, and country. We then slowly folded and handed the flag to the widow. After that we got back on the bus and headed back to Ft. Polk. The sergeant and first lieutenant were joking about who was going to take the widow out that

ARMY DAYS

night as she now had the $10,000 life insurance. I thought that was a pretty low comment; or was it their way of dealing with the reality of what had happened? Is life and death just a piece of film that you are viewing as it happens and then you display the emotions you feel in a way that seems appropriate for the situation? Or maybe by showing your true emotion you are afraid of being vulnerable thereby you choose an emotion that keeps you safe.

After basic training, my next stop was Ft. Sill, Oklahoma, where I went to school for ballistic meteorology even though I had requested to be an airport controller. If the Army didn't need you for what you had signed up for, they put you into a similar classification. Soon, I realized this new field would be better than being in the infantry, slogging through the rice paddies and jungle.

I learned that we would be sending up weather balloons with a transmitter attached to them that would send back signals. Tracking them with our radar would give us wind speed and direction, as well as humidity and temperature at different elevations in the atmosphere. You would take all this information to the fire direction control (FDC) for the artillery batteries. This would allow them to adjust the artillery according to the wind speed and direction along with density and temperatures so that the artillery round would land on target and not on our troops. The information you provided to the FDC had to be accurate and timely.

Ft. Sill was a better duty station than Ft. Polk; they even had a movie theater on post. At Ft. Sill, we were served better food and more of it as we were not in basic training anymore—we were not trying to become lean and mean. The sergeant in charge of the mess hall would have you sign in as you were

RANDOM TANGENTS

lining up for chow and sometimes you would sign the roster two or three times so he could draw more rations. Just a way of getting a little extra for the soldiers he was feeding.

We had more time off and could often go off post on weekends. It seemed like military bases at that time were notorious for having a town nearby that offered booze and ladies, especially at the end of the month when the soldiers got paid. I heard stories about guys losing or spending all their money at these places in short order, so I never went.

After graduating from the meteorology school, I had leave to go home for a couple of weeks before I had to report to Oakland, California. I visited with friends and family before leaving to head back. The night before reporting to Oakland, I stayed in San Francisco and found a little bar called Sam's. It had 101 different kinds of beer, mostly on tap, and I decided I was going to try most of them. The next morning, I was hardly functional.

I did make it to Oakland, where they issued us jungle fatigues and then loaded us onto a World Airways jet. They flew us to Anchorage, Alaska, where it was a brisk 35 degrees outside as we unloaded while they refueled the plane. Our next stop was Guam, where it was raining by the buckets as we deplaned for refueling. The final stop was Bien Hoa airbase in Vietnam. As soon as we came to a stop, they opened the doors and started shouting for us to quickly get the hell out of the plane as rockets were coming in. It was now June of 1969 and we were having a sudden wake-up call to a new reality. Welcome to Vietnam!

The heat and humidity combined were like walking into a blast furnace; you were saturated in minutes with your own sweat. We were taken over to Long Binh for processing, which

ARMY DAYS

took three days. The sleeping accommodations were in a barracks-style building with three-inch cotton mattresses on wire-spring cots. With such a big turnover of guys coming through here, the mattresses had been soaked and stained with a lot of guys' sweat. I decided to sleep under the stars and forego the luxury accommodation inside the barracks. Sleeping under the stars on a clear night takes you away from the present moment and transports you into another dimension—to the world of infinite possibilities. At that moment it was an escape from the harsh reality of where I was.

One day I had to go on a detail to pick up some supplies from another area. We were riding along in a truck, and the guy who was stationed there grabbed a broom and started swinging at Vietnamese guys riding on bicycles, trying to knock them off. I thought, "Is this what it is all about? Making people hate you?" Why this individual had to take out his hatred or frustrations on innocent people I didn't comprehend, but I was new in this country and the war.

In time I could see that some soldiers had seen too much death and did not know who they could trust anymore, so they started to hate all Vietnamese. Psychologically you build a profile of the enemy in your mind and think of them as less than human, which makes it easier for you to kill them. The Vietnamese started to look alike, your hatred boiled over, and you did what you normally wouldn't.

They gave us a fluoride treatment for our teeth, shots for whatever, and told us to make sure we took our malaria pills every day. All the time I was there, I never took any of the malaria pills. The two guys on either side of me in the hooch came down with malaria even though they had been taking their pills. I guess it is the luck of the draw. After getting back

RANDOM TANGENTS

stateside, one of the guys I knew came down with malaria ninety days after he returned. They said it could stay in your system and lay dormant for up to three months, and they were right.

While there we also learned how to repel off towers with ropes in case we needed to repel out of helicopters. On the third day we were called out into formation and they started calling names out for assignment to certain divisions. 1st Calvary Division (Airmobile), here I come! Two of guys who I had been at school with at Ft. Sill were also called for the 1st Calvary Division (Airmobile). It was called Airmobile because the 1st Cav used helicopters for the assault on enemy forces. We were told we were going up to Phouc Vinh, which was not thought to be a very good spot as it got hit quite often. Great news!

We boarded a small caribou plane, lifted off and landed shortly at Phouc Vinh. We reported to headquarters of the division artillery and were informed that we were going on up to Quan Loi to a small unit there. The guys in Phouc Vinh were telling us that Quan Loi was nicknamed "rocket city" as rockets were coming in almost every day. We got issued our rifles, clips, ammo, and a flak jacket before boarding the C-123 plane to go on to Quan Loi. It was now June of 1969.

CHAPTER FOUR
Quan Loi

Less than a week after arriving at Quan Loi, one of the two guys who flew up with us was sent back to be a clerk in Phouc Vinh. It seemed he had kissed some bum and told them how educated and great he was while we were in Phouc Vinh for that short period of time on our way to Quan Loi. He must have been sweating bullets knowing where he was going and made the pitch. He was all about himself; being put in a dangerous situation for his country was not to his liking. I was glad he was gone, as I wouldn't have been able to depend on him in a firefight.

Two of the guys in our outfit left shortly after I arrived as part of the troop rotation. One of these guys, Ed, had extended his stay by six months so he would have enough money to buy a new GTO when he got back home. I thought it was a little crazy to put your life on the line for another six months just for a car. He had sent all his money home to his parents to save it for him. After he arrived home, we found out that his parents had spent all his money. How could his parents do something like that?

The other guy named Larry got one of those "Dear John" letters from his wife a month before he was supposed to return home. It turned out that she had filed for divorce, so he had nothing to return to—no wife, no money, and no hero's welcome. He had spent a year putting his life on the line while living in a hellhole. He spent his last four weeks hugging a beer can, trying to medicate his depression. These were just a couple of the many sad stories that I heard while there.

Quan Loi was situated not far from a small Vietnamese village named An Loc, just ten miles from the Cambodian border. This area of Cambodia protruding into Vietnam was called the "fishhook," and it was where much of the infiltration from the Ho Chi Minh Trail entered Vietnam. Quan Loi was a firebase from which several Army units operated.

They said that the Quan Loi airstrip had been a golf course owned by a Frenchman who had a rubber plantation in the Central Highlands. As far as I knew, the rubber plantation was still in operation; I heard the U.S. paid him for any rubber trees we destroyed while driving our tanks through the area. It was supposed to be all part of the Michelin rubber plantation, but who knows the real story? The Frenchman wasn't living there at the time, but I did see his private plane fly in once. I heard his Vietnamese servant happened to walk into the prop of the plane as it taxied to a stop; that ended the servant's life quickly.

I arrived in June and during the first six months there, we were hit with rockets almost every day. In May, before I arrived, they had a ground attack and lost a mortar platoon as a Viet Cong (VC) sapper tossed a satchel charge into their bunker at night. Sappers were highly trained enemy demolition personnel that used satchel charges as one of their primary weapons once they infiltrated the perimeter. I was told that after the attack we collected the enemy dead, one of whom was their barber, and dumped their bodies in the town square of An Loc. It was our way of letting the locals know we didn't take prisoners when they came through our wire at night to kill

QUAN LOI

us, especially locals who worked on our firebase for us during the day. When I went to get a haircut on our base for the first time, I was worried when the new barber, who was taking the place of the one we killed, brought out a straight razor to shave my neck. Trust is a precious thing that is hard to earn in a war zone.

When I arrived, the 1st Infantry Division was moving out of the firebase and the 1st Cavalry Division was moving in. As the 1st Cav moved in they bulldozed the whole perimeter around the firebase and installed new concertina wire and bunkers to enhance security. The perimeter then was flown over by helicopters spraying a "defoliant" to kill the vegetation.

Our small unit of thirteen men consisted of a warrant officer in charge, four non-commissioned officers (NCOs), and eight specialists of which I was one. We worked in twelve-hour shifts seven days a week sounding the atmosphere. The atmospheric sounding was performed every six hours to collect information for the artillery batteries on our firebase, other firebases, and landing zones (LZs) that were in the surrounding area. When our team was on day shift, we started at 6:00 a.m. to perform our first sounding and followed up with our second sounding at noon. Between soundings and until late afternoon, we would fill sandbags, ammo boxes, and powder canisters with dirt. We used all of these to provide blast walls and tops for our bunkers in case of incoming rockets or mortars. We were always upgrading and building something just to keep us busy.

We traded shifts every month, so you shared day and night shifts with the rest of the guys in the unit. When on day shift, we would take turns pulling bunker guard on the perimeter. One thing about pulling bunker guard was that nobody screwed with you. In fact, I offered to pull it full time but that didn't work. We would joke to one another about having to do something we didn't want to and say, "What are they going to do to me, send me to Nam?" It was our way of releasing tension.

The ballistic meteorology messages had to be delivered every six hours to all the artillery batteries. It took an hour to compute the data before delivering it and the midnight sounding message was probably the most dangerous to deliver. I found out as I was driving our three-quarter-ton vehicle to deliver the message at 1:00 a.m. one morning when the VC decided to zero their mortar tube in on my headlights. The first mortar hit a partially full JP-4 jet and helicopter fuel bladder as I drove by. It went up in a ball of smoke and fire, and I quickly turned off the headlights, drove the truck into the ditch, and jumped out. I waited a few minutes to see if there were any more rounds coming in before I crawled back into the truck to continue. I took off again with just my running lights on, but the pickup was still visible, so in came some more rounds close to where our mortar platoon was. I drove the rest of the way with no headlights on. By driving with the door open, I could see the road alongside me. It took a little bit longer to deliver the messages, but it was much safer.

Our operations bunker was only about eighty yards from the perimeter of the firebase and our balloon inflation shack was only seventy yards away. As you could imagine, we were always a little gun shy going out at midnight and sending up a sounding balloon, as we had to shine a spotlight on the balloon as we released it so we could visually lock on to it with our radar. A couple of times, we had guys on the bunkers shoot a tracer round through the hydrogen-filled balloon and light it

QUAN LOI

up. It wasn't funny for us as it took another hour to get another one ready, thus delaying the delivery of critical information.

On my birthday, August 12, 1969, we were told that there was a high probability that we could come under attack that evening and were told to prepare and to stay alert. My plan was to do a little birthday celebration but that was postponed. Now we were all making sure our weapons were at the ready as we turned in for the night. Before midnight, all hell broke loose as the VC sappers blew open our wire and came through on both sides of the firebase. The Cobra gunships quickly got in the air to provide air support as artillery shrapnel and illumination rounds were directed in from other LZs close to us. Our own mortar platoons were bringing in mortars as close as they could and provided illumination rounds to keep the area lit. Our team stayed at the edge of our area, protecting it against any infiltration from the perimeter, or green line as we called it. On one side of us was the 6/27th Artillery Battery which had their bunkers and cyclone fence separating them from the perimeter. On the other side of us was the 11th Armored Cavalry and their armor. Some of the bunkers were overrun on the perimeter at first, but the 11th Armored Cavalry quickly responded with their tanks. They also brought down the "quad-50," a five-ton truck with four .50-caliber machine guns mounted in the back. They strafed the whole area, and anything that was hit was history. Soon there were planes dropping large illumination flares around the whole firebase. It was almost like daylight and stayed that way until morning. Finally, at daylight, there were still a few enemy soldiers inside our perimeter who were taken care of as we finished securing the area.

On the other side of our firebase, the VC infiltrated further into the headquarters area; a lot of close-in fighting took

RANDOM TANGENTS

place there. We were finally were able to drive them out and take back control. At daylight, a fixed-wing aircraft we called "spooky," aka Puff the magic dragon, circled our firebase with miniguns firing thousands of rounds of ammunition beyond our perimeter taking care of any remaining VC. After that the F-4 phantom jets came in with napalm and dropped their loads outside our perimeter to incinerate the area.

That morning after the attack, as I walked down to the perimeter road, I saw a tank doing a donut turn on top of a dead VC. He was just some ground-up meat with a patch of black hair. Then an armored personnel carrier (APC) drove by with a dead enemy strapped to the front as a hood ornament. Inside our perimeter wire, there were dead enemy lying all over. A lot of them had limbs missing and were cut into pieces due to the .50-caliber machine guns that strafed the area. They didn't look real. One guy was cutting off ammo belts from the gray, rubbery remains. Many of the bodies looked very young, but it was better not to think about it. They were your enemy, they had weapons, and they were trying to kill you. The smell of death was everywhere; a smell one can never forget! The value of human life seemed so low at this point. A loader and dump truck showed up to start cleaning up the area as I headed back up to our compound. We read that we lost over fifty soldiers during the battle that night in this sector of Vietnam and the total enemy body count was over 450.

That evening I was going to celebrate my birthday a day late. I was still in one piece and glad to be alive. I usually stocked up on three or four cases of Hamm's beer as it was only $2.40/case and the light aluminum cans made it easy to cool down. We had a blood bank cooler in our operations bunker; they were used to transport blood across Vietnam. It was a big foam chest that we could put three cases of beer in along with a big block of ice and it would keep for several days. At this time, we didn't have any ice so I decided to borrow a big CO2 fire extinguisher on a dolly from the 6/27th artillery to cool down my birthday beer. I put the case of beer in the cooler and turned on the fire extinguisher. The noise was a bit loud, more like a jet engine, and it took a lot of force to keep the lid from flying off the chest.

Next thing I heard was a male voice from behind me. "Soldier, what do you think you are doing?"

"Cooling my beer, Sir!" I answered immediately.

"Is that what that fire extinguisher is for, soldier?"

"No, Sir!"

"If I were you, I would expedite the return of it ASAP, do you understand?"

"Yes, Sir!"

As the lieutenant turned around and left, I quickly wheeled the fire extinguisher back over to the artillery bunker from which it came. Luckily, my beer was cool enough to drink, and I proceeded to indulge heavily as I was off duty that evening.

Christmas was coming up and we were all getting packages from back home. My twin brothers had sent me a bottle of Chivas Regal Scotch inside a round oatmeal box packed with popcorn to keep it from breaking. Damn, was that good! I made it (the Scotch, not the popcorn!) last for a week or so. My neighbor across the street from back home sent a fruitcake he made himself, and it was so saturated with rum you could eat it or wring the rum out and drink it. It was pretty tasty! These care packages meant everything to the guys over there. It was a chance to take a little time away from war and think about family and close friendships that you had back home. You knew you were in their thoughts.

RANDOM TANGENTS

However, not all packages lifted my mood. I was interested in a beautiful young lady with red hair when I left for Vietnam. We were childhood friends; we grew up together. Before I left, I stopped by to see her at college to say goodbye. At Christmas I received a Christmas card from her with just her name signed at the bottom. No letter, no "How are you doing?"—just a signed card. It was sort of a downer, but life goes on. Mine and hers, too—only separately.

On New Year's Eve we all got together and one of the guys had a reel-to-reel tape player with some music. A few days prior to that, one of the sergeants in our outfit, Billy, had taken our orders for some hard liquor and picked it up while down at the Long Binh base exchange. We had plenty to drink and celebrated just being alive. We even gave our dog some beer in a bowl, and after a while it couldn't stand up. We laughed as we weren't doing much better.

There were two guys that I trusted with my life and one was Billy, the sergeant who was a full-blood Choctaw Indian from Talihina, Oklahoma. He was easygoing, a lifer in the Army. He didn't say much, but our friendship didn't need a lot of words. The other guy was David, who was on the same team as Billy and me. David had been a member of the National Association of Intercollegiate Athletics (NAIA) All-American Gymnastics Team in college and was like a human spring. He was from Gilmer, Texas, and, of course, had a real Texan sense of humor. We depended on each other in a place far from the reality we knew back home.

Since we were so close to the Cambodian border and the Ho Chi Minh Trail, we had Special Forces working from our firebase. I noticed one day that they had some Hmong mercenaries with them. The Hmong mercenaries got paid for the

QUAN LOI

ears of the enemy that they brought back from their incursions into Cambodia and Laos. After a while ears didn't suffice and heads started to be counted. This was supported by the CIA and Air America, who were flying into areas the regular Army couldn't. The head of the Hmong mercenaries had a camp that was finally napalmed by us as his tactics were getting out of hand—or so the story goes. This whole story reminds me of the movie *Apocalypse Now*. Today there are Hmong settlements in the United States as many fled their country after the war in fear of retaliation by the VC and North Vietnamese Army. The large number of casualties the Hmong fighters suffered started showing at the end of the war when the only fighters left were young boys. For them it was a gruesome war, death was their business every day.

Most people in the U.S. don't know what goes on behind the scenes as war plays out. It is something normal U.S. citizens can't fathom; the atrocities of war are so far from your doorstep that they don't matter. War is not cut and dried. Foot soldiers don't know how money and power enter into the whole scenario; they are just expendable numbers supposedly fighting for a just cause. Is the media guilty of sheltering the American public from what is really going on or is the real truth being held back from the media?

The 1st Air Cavalry had special decks of cards made up with their logo on one side saying, "Death from Above." They would leave these cards on dead enemy and all around the villages they passed through. The VC were superstitious; these cards were a bad omen. Some customized decks of cards were made that only had the ace of spades on the opposite side, which was also considered a bad omen. Our psychological warfare included dropping millions of pamphlets and flyers

RANDOM TANGENTS

into North Vietnam telling about the Chieu Hoi (Open Arms) program, which encouraged the VC to surrender in order to be welcomed back by their brothers in South Vietnam. This was the most extensive psychological program aimed at North Vietnam for more than ten years. In the end, when you are not allowed to win, and you are faced with boundaries you cannot cross, the effects of the never-ending wait to get attacked starts affecting you psychologically. As you go through the villages or cities, you can't tell a friend from an enemy. You can only be sure when they ambush you in the jungle or try to overrun your firebase or LZ at night.

During the dry season, the dust was two to three inches thick wherever there was traffic—foot or vehicle. We would work all day sweating and take a shower before turning in at night. Our shower was a 300-gallon tank of water with a gasoline-fueled burner attached to it to heat the water. We would have to take a water truck down to the water point and fill it so we could then fill our shower tank. Once the water tank was filled, one of us would fill the tank for the heater with gasoline and start it up to heat the water. Below the tank was a wooden shower stall and a shower head. It was always a treat to get all the reddish dirt washed off you. Your "tan" disappeared down the drain every day.

One day I had just filled the tank with gasoline and turned the fuel tank on. I lit a match to start it up and suddenly fuel tank caught on fire. Thinking it was going to blow up, I grabbed it as quickly as I could and threw it on the ground. One of the guys quickly grabbed a fire extinguisher and put it out. To be honest, these heaters were designed to be used in the kitchen mess hall to heat water; they were dangerous.

QUAN LOI

Our hooch, where we slept on cots, had a four-foot blast wall around it with screen wire above to allow air circulation. The top was just an old canvas tent and was good enough to keep you dry. Your cot also had a mosquito net over it to protect you from the malaria the mosquitoes carried. You usually covered up with a poncho liner just to have something light over you to keep the chill off.

One night I felt something crawl under my poncho liner on my chest and then all the way down to my feet. I froze. I realized it was a rat and I didn't want it to bite me. Once it came out from under my covers, I shot out of bed and turned my flashlight on. It scurried out the back door and all the cockroaches ran to find cracks in the floor so they could disappear as well. Instances like this only made you dream that much more of being back stateside in your own bed.

As the rats were becoming a problem, we had a Montagnard man set some rat traps around our hooch. One day he pulled out a rat with a big smile on his face; he was going to take it home for supper. It probably tasted like chicken! One man's nuisance is another man's treasure, seemingly.

A few nights later, when I thought the rat issue was behind me, a cobra snake slithered out between some stacked powder canisters that were filled with dirt in the wall of our operations bunker. One of the guys, in all his brilliance, opened fire with his M-16. Rounds were flying everywhere, hitting our equipment, and putting holes in it. Miraculously, none of the rounds hit any of our crew. That guy's IQ had to be about three points below plant level. At least he got the snake.

One day I was across the airstrip from our small compound delivering a message when a few mortars came in. When I got back to our side of the runway the incoming mortar rounds had landed close to our area. David said to me that we should probably sleep in the bunker tonight as the VC were zeroing in for the night bombardment. I wasn't looking forward to sleeping in a rat-infested bunker, but he finally convinced me it was the safest place to be. About midnight the mortars came in, and it was a good thing we were in the bunker. The next morning, we saw that a mortar had hit the tree branches above our hooch, which caused an air burst with shrapnel going everywhere. Both of our cots were full of holes and the old canvas cover over the hooch wasn't going to keep out much rain from then on. We quickly put a new tin roof over our sleeping area.

During my time over there I got to know quite a lot about the guys I was with since we were together most of the time. You know about their wives or girlfriends back home and how they deal with being away for so long. One guy in our crew named Tim had a beautiful girlfriend in California who would send him these fantastic letters. She would write a letter on a balloon, then deflate it and send it. She also wrote letters on popsicle sticks with numbers on the ends of them, so he could put them in order to read the message. To everyone's surprise, on his last visit home, he ended the relationship. He had already spent eighteen months over there and had extended for another six months when he went home on leave. I believe during his time at home he had a hard time dealing with reality—or maybe his girlfriend had enough. I can't blame her. When he came back he started spending a lot of his free time with a local Vietnamese girl from An Loc and was always trying to help out her family and local villagers. One had to understand the mindset of these people as they had been at war for over forty years and their main thought was to survive as a family unit any way they could.

QUAN LOI

One day Tim asked me to buy a watch for him over at the post exchange (PX) as he had used up his ration card for watch purchases. I agreed since he was leaving soon, and I thought he was purchasing it for someone back home. The PX was located on the opposite side of the runway and it was where we got our beer, watches, cameras, and tape players if the convoy made it up to the firebase. A couple of days later, the military police came to our unit. They had found the watch I purchased on the young Vietnamese lady leaving our post. I told them the truth and didn't hear any more about it. I imagine they thought either she had stolen it, or she was going to sell it on the black market.

It was good that Tim finally went home after spending two years there, as reality seemed to be slowly disappearing for him. He was the only guy I knew who could sit up and sleep with his eyes open. I think the longer one spends in a war zone, the more one becomes disconnected from the value system that exists back home. Within a week of his leaving, I saw this young Vietnamese lady with a first lieutenant on the other side of our firebase. Time goes on.

Soldiers continually rotated in and out of country; short timers left, and greenies showed up. While there, we got a new warrant officer and a sergeant, both about the same time. After being there for a week the sergeant told me that our perimeter was in good shape and asked if we were using tractors to keep the overgrowth down. I told him we kept it clean using artillery and mortar rounds mixed with a little bit of Agent Orange. I assured him that if he stuck around for a while, he would find out.

The top sergeant in our outfit was an alcoholic and a dick—not a good combination for a leader in our small unit. Once

RANDOM TANGENTS

someone put a hand grenade under his pillow on his cot. When he picked the pillow up to go to bed, the handle flew off the hand grenade, which means you have five seconds before it goes off. The sergeant shat himself as he didn't know that the firing cap had been removed, making it a dud. Nobody knew who placed that hand grenade under his pillow, but the sergeant came away with a whole different attitude from then on. He no longer screwed with the guys making up things for them to do while he kept his drinking buddies off the duty roster and pulling perimeter guard.

With fifty-seven days left before I was to leave Vietnam, I hopped on a chopper down to Bien Hoa and over to the 1st Cavalry Division Headquarters in Long Binh. I put in for an extension to stay another thirty days in country so that when I returned stateside, I wouldn't have to be reassigned to another duty post and be discharged, but I missed the cut-off date by three days. When I look back, that was probably a good thing.

Coming in from the field, you always carried your M-16 and ammo belt. In Long Binh, I noticed most of the soldiers stationed there didn't carry weapons and wore nice clean fatigues. Another thing I noticed was that by looking at the soldiers' boots and fatigues coming in from the field, you could tell approximately what part of country they had come from. Quan Loi had a red dirt, while Song Be had a grayer dirt.

I couldn't believe that at the Long Binh base, the Air Force had a movie theater with hamburgers, real milkshakes, and popcorn. That is something you dreamt about up where I was at. When the siren went off signaling incoming rockets or mortars, everyone would run for a bunker. Hell, the rockets could be landing a mile away, so I would keep walking—not worrying unless it started to get closer. After almost a year in Vietnam I

QUAN LOI

had been conditioned to the sound of incoming; at this point it was all about perspective.

The guy I was traveling with and I decided to grab a beer before catching a chopper back and stopped by the 101st Airborne's enlisted men's (EM) bar. We went in and ordered a beer at the bar and started to drink when a sergeant came up and told us we would have to drink outside since we weren't 101st Airborne. Okay, no problem! Then he went down to the next fellow who had a 1st Cav patch on his sleeve and started to say something to him but stopped. On the other sleeve was a Special Forces patch and a beret in his pants pocket so the sergeant quickly welcomed him as an airborne brother. The sergeant dug into his pocket for some money and said the beer was on him.

I realized I was becoming a short timer, with only a few weeks left in country, and all I was thinking about was getting on the plane to go back home. Most of the guys in my outfit now were newbies in country and hadn't been around many mortar or rocket attacks. Just a week before I left, I was sitting and talking to some of the new guys when a rocket came in. As soon as I heard it, I was on the floor in a heartbeat. The new guys were still sitting and looking down at me when the rocket went off some distance away. I told them they should start practicing hugging the ground when they heard that sound if they wanted to increase their odds of staying alive.

I received a two-week early departure date and headed to Long Binh to process out of country. While there I talked with a major who asked if I wanted to take an R & R, (short for rest and relaxation) before going home since I hadn't had one. My reply? I just wanted to go home. The armed services had places

RANDOM TANGENTS

set up where soldiers could go for a week for R&R. You were furnished a roundtrip plane ride to places like Bangkok, Kuala Lumpur, Singapore, and Taipei, which were popular for single guys. These places had areas set up with plenty of working girls and bars. If you wished to go to Hawaii to meet your wife, that was also an option.

Most of the guys in my unit received their R&Rs during their tour. I remember one of them came back from Bangkok with a pair of panties on top of his camouflage helmet just to show off. The pictures they brought back from their R&R showed attractive young ladies who they stayed with for the week they were there. Knowing one had to come back to Vietnam, one lived it up as it might have been your last chance.

I got bored waiting for my flight back to the States and hopped on a chopper back up to Quan Loi for a day to see the guys one last time. While I was in Quan Loi, I noticed the officer and sergeant in charge of the unit had the guys painting the metal siding on the new operations bunker they had built. The new bunker was within fifty yards of the perimeter and on the side of the hill. The paint was a nice bright silver so as the moon came up, it was like a bullseye for the VC. I told them what I thought before I left as they couldn't do anything to me then. In fact, the first time they built the new bunker, before I left initially, they stacked empty 105mm ammo boxes filled with dirt on top for protection. When the whole bunker collapsed before they finished, it turned out that two of the ammo boxes on the roof still had live rounds in them. A minor oversight with major consequences! Boy was I glad to be going home.

Small oversights such as these even more solidified the need for new officers and leaders in the war zone, to be

QUAN LOI

mentored during their transition from some of the vets who have been there for a while. The officer in charge thought we were in a secure area and was going to paint everything up nice and pretty. He was, in fact, waving a red flag in front of Charlie and giving him a target for his mortars.

There were many soldiers over there who had it worse than I did, and a lot didn't make it back either. After a while, being over there under those circumstances, your value of life starts changing. I got to a point where I quit thinking about making it back and only thought about making it through another day. It was when I only had a couple of weeks left in country and knew I was heading home that my values started changing back to normal—whatever that is. You can only stay wound tight for so long; your thoughts and value systems change as you exist day to day. Deep inside you want to make it back but there is always the chance that you won't.

QUAN LOI MAP

RANDOM TANGENTS

DEATH CARD

OUR HOOCH

QUAN LOI

4TH OF JULY BAR-B-Q

AUTHOR AFTER HARD DAY'S WORK

RANDOM TANGENTS

AUTHOR IN OPERATIONS BUNKER

CHAPTER FIVE
Homeward Bound

I noticed on our flight back to the U.S. that all the stewardesses were old enough to be my mother and I thought that was probably wise with a group of 200 soldiers. Also, there was no alcohol on board, so we had a non-eventful flight and landed safely on U.S. soil at Oakland, California. When stepping off the plane onto the tarmac, you were finally able to release that last bit of tension as you knew you were safely back home. It was like breathing again after holding your breath for a year—the tension was leaving but now you had to deal with the memories.

After landing in Oakland, we processed through a building where they gave you Army clothes to travel in, and you had the option to get rid of anything that you didn't want. I didn't think twice as I tossed all my jungle fatigues, boots, and unnecessary clothes. I didn't want to be reminded of Vietnam ever again. The next stop was the Oakland airport to catch a plane back to a place close to home. While waiting at the airport, I spent some time in the USO Club. They had some coffee, snacks, and cots to lie down on. One of the soldiers catching some sleep was having a nightmare, and the older lady that worked at the club went over and touched him to wake him up. No sooner then she could take her next breath he had her by the throat before he realized where he was. In her shock she turned and ran as fast as she could to get help. The MPs were on their way to deal with this guy but before they reached the door I stopped them. I believe they understood once I explained he was in Special Forces and had just came back. They decided to let it go as they had a level of understanding about what had transpired. They calmed the lady down and talked to the soldier in a caring manor and welcomed him home.

As a specialist fourth class my base pay was $140 a month, which I saved and sent home ahead of me. On top of that phenomenal sum of money I received $70 per month combat pay along with a free $10,000 life insurance policy while there. The $70 a month I used to pay for basic things like Hamm's beer, and $15 a month went to the Vietnamese woman who cleaned our hooch and did our laundry.

I had enough money on me when I landed in Oakland to buy a plane ticket to St. Louis and from there, I took a Greyhound bus to Decatur, Illinois. Once in Decatur, I had $2.50 left in my pocket, so I flagged down a taxi and asked him if $2.50 would get me out to the highway. He told me to hop in and gave me a ride out to the highway. I thought I would hitchhike the last fifteen miles home, hoping that with the Army greens on, it wouldn't be long before I could get a ride, but I was in for a surprise. When I finally did get a ride, I was dropped off alongside the highway in downtown Dalton City just two blocks from home. It was a weird feeling being back and walking down the street to get home. Memories of sidewalks, streets, houses, green grass, and the smell of fresh air after a gentle rain were all coming back. A year had disappeared, a chunk of my life gone, and a memory of that year that would never leave me.

As I walked up into our yard, our old dog came running down and started barking at me. As soon as I called his name,

HOMEWARD BOUND

he went into a skid and then started jumping up and down. I walked into the house, as we never locked our homes or our cars out in the country. My mother was vacuuming the carpet; she didn't hear me come in. No one knew I was coming home early, so it was quite the surprise—we embraced and tears trickled down my mother's cheeks. Being home, a place you never thought much about, was now a welcome refuge from what I'd left behind. Just being with the ones you love helps start the transition back to some sort of normality.

Father came home later, and we hugged and talked a bit, but not about the war. I told him I wanted to throw a party and invite the neighbors, so that's what we did. We had one heck of a shindig with a horse-watering tank full of beer and ice along with rib-eye steaks on the grill. The neighbor across the street brought over a bottle of scotch and I polished that off before the night was over.

There was an old Harley-Davidson sitting in our workshop that my father had purchased. Before leaving to go to Vietnam, motorcycles were something that weren't mentioned as wanting as my mother's brother had been killed on one. Now not only did my father have one but two of my brothers also owned them. I borrowed my father's motorcycle to take it for a ride and maybe stop by and see an old girlfriend. On the second day when I was riding it, an older lady in a big old car pulled right out in front of me as I was going down the highway. I had to stand up and put all the force I could on those brakes to make that damn motorcycle stop. After that, I rode it home and parked it. I had dodged death for a year, and I wasn't going to get killed on a motorcycle the first week I got back.

The money that I had saved in an accrual account while in Vietnam was waiting for me at home. This money I used to

RANDOM TANGENTS

purchase a used MGB convertible which was a little four-cylinder sports car. It was a lot of fun to drive—especially in the summertime. After paying for it I still had $900 left that I spent drinking during the rest of my thirty-day leave. It was mostly scotch on the rocks every night until the bar closed in Decatur. I would get home at about 2:00 a.m., sleep in, and do it all over again the next night. I wanted to stay numb, forget about the past, and unwind. Being under a constant threat of being killed at any moment, one is like a tight spring and needs time to uncoil, relax, and try to grasp your forgotten reality. By the time I was heading to my next duty station, I was spitting blood and knew I had reached my limits on drinking; it wasn't solving anything.

Before I left to go back to the Army for my last five months, I took almost everything I had brought back from Vietnam (which wasn't much) and burned it. We had a big burning hole for trash on the farm; I threw everything into the hole and lit it up with the help of a little gasoline. The only thing I kept was a bunch of Kodachrome slides that I had taken of some beautiful sunrises and sunsets. That was my way of forgetting and burying the Vietnam experience. The closure was helped by the scotch too!

To be truthful, you can't turn the memories off like a faucet. But you must try not to relive them every day of your life, thereby not letting the trauma grab your soul. As soon as I got to my next duty post and started hearing helicopters, all my Vietnam memories came flooding back. Fifty years later, I am writing this next to a runway used by the Air Force. I see and hear C-130s and helicopters come in and take off frequently. Yes, the sounds still bring up the memories, but you learn to brush them off and go on. The only thing that still sets me off is unexpected loud noises; it is a reflex action that is hard to control as you tense up in fight-or-flight mode.

For years, I never talked about Vietnam. Then one day, when my daughter was twenty-eight years old, she asked me why I never said anything about the things that had happened over there; she wanted to know about it. It is hard to open up about these memories as war is insane. I told her I would only tell her one time about what I saw and what I felt. Later she was in tears, just like me. People who have never experienced war will never know what it is like as words can't describe it and the impact it has on you for the rest of your life. I had a Zippo cigarette lighter I carried for a while in Vietnam, which was engraved with the phrase: "For those who have faced death, life has a flavor the protected will never know."

For the last five months of my obligation, I was stationed at Ft. Carson, next to Colorado Springs. Most of the guys there were beer drinkers, so we would go to Pueblo, Colorado, on weekends to drink some beer and listen to music. I could handle the beer, but scotch was out of the question. There were other guys in the barracks who were dopers and would head up to Boulder to get their LSD, magic mushrooms, marijuana, or whatever drug they could get their hands on. At the height of the flower-power era, drugs were easy to come by.

While at Ft. Carson, I enrolled in a project transition course with Firestone Tire and Rubber, which lasted for two months. The course was supposed to help you get back into the workforce. It taught you everything about tires and dealerships. I graduated at the top of the class, so I thought I had a good chance to get a halfway-decent job with them when I got out.

RANDOM TANGENTS

The soldiers coming back from Vietnam weren't treated as heroes or warriors like they are today. People didn't want to know about the war, and the returning soldiers had to hold a lot inside without anyone to talk to about it. There was little help for them when they needed it most. Some of my high school friends came back all messed up with everything they saw and did. Later on, cancer ate up most of them. Agent Orange probably figured into it to some degree as well as the psychological disease they held inside.

Years later I received a phone call from the wife of one of my best friends in high school. He had just passed away from cancer at the age of forty-five. He had been in Vietnam and came back a little sickly but didn't think anything of it as he raised his family. I always called them just before Christmas every year to see how they were doing.

When I made the call that November, his wife answered and said she was afraid I was going to call. In tears, she told me that he had cancer and was in the hospital. Two days later I drove to Illinois to see him. It was sad to see a guy who was six feet tall and used to weigh 210 lbs. all shriveled up in a hospital bed only weighing 150 lbs. They were feeding him through a tube as they had run chemo through him and radiated him so much that his stomach and intestines were pretty much fried into a large gray mass. After charging his insurance company $250,000, the doctors told him they had done all they could, and the rest was up to him. I get upset when I think about how many of the guys returning from Vietnam were coming down with cancer and other maladies from Agent Orange.

One of my closest friends in Vietnam, David, wrote *I Remember Quan Loi* on his experiences trying to come to terms with the inner turmoil he carried. He told me how hard it was for him to put it into words. We reconnected two years ago when I flew down to Shreveport to see him. We spent three days visiting and catching up and at times talked about Vietnam and what we had experienced. It was a conversation that only he and I could have since we understood each other's thoughts and feelings during that time and place. He sadly passed away in January of 2019 with lung cancer. Was it due to Agent Orange? Who knows? At least now, after years of political battle, veterans who were exposed to Agent Orange have some financial assistance if they are diagnosed with certain ailments.

Years later I came to understand that during my time in Vietnam I never really feared death; it's something that just happens. I never thought of being scared as my service was a duty I had to perform—hopefully I would come out of it. You follow the script and if it is your time to go, that is just the way it is. Of course, you try to make all the right decisions about staying alive while doing your utmost to perform your duties under tenuous circumstances. Others depend on you as you depend on them in the hopes that everyone gets to go home alive to their family and loved ones. War is not a game!

Think about this! Our country's economy is based on war. President Dwight D. Eisenhower warned us of this in a speech on January 17, 1961. He warned against the rise of the military industrial complex and its growth getting out of control. He also said that with the abuse of power, we would be in never-ending wars. President Eisenhower kept us out of war for eight years he was in office and our economy prospered with the new interstate highway system. And where are we now? Today, our roads, bridges, and dams are in need of urgent repair and we are still fighting wars.

CHAPTER SIX
The American Dream

It was the end of 1970; I was finally out of the Army, and it was time to look for a job. I went to Denver and interviewed with Firestone Tire and Rubber. Their offer to me was to start busting tires at $120 per week and then work my way up in the company. That wasn't going to work for me; I had more ambition and knew I could make more money working in construction.

The next stop was the veterans' representative down at the unemployment office. I interviewed with him for five minutes before he looked at me and said, "I see guys like you in here every day with a couple of years of college wanting a good job, and I know you will be back here in a week begging for a dishwashing job." That didn't sit right with me, either, but this was the way things were at that time and place.

I started looking for construction jobs and found two. One was a concrete form setter job for housing foundations, but it was already December and I knew that winter probably wasn't going to provide steady work. I ended up taking a job at a construction site at the Mountain Bell telephone building. I told the construction superintendent that I had just gotten out of the Army, had construction experience, and needed a job. He offered me a laborer's job for $3.75 per hour, which would last through the winter as it was mostly inside work.

THE AMERICAN DREAM

The construction company was owned by Gerald H. Phipps, who owned the Denver Broncos at that time. (I found this out later when we had to go and erect the temporary stands at the old Mile High Stadium.) I would come to know, and like, this company over the years ahead.

I rented a sleeping room from an older couple about six blocks away from the jobsite for $10 a week. Life was good! I started being a little bit of a hippie with longer hair and granny glasses as well as listening to Led Zeppelin, Santana, and Pink Floyd. Beer was the drink of choice as you could get a draft beer for a quarter in most of Denver at that time. There was one bar called Doc's, where an eight-ounce Coors was fifteen cents. Everyone went to that bar at the end of the month when money was running short. Being from a farm town in Illinois, I didn't know much about Mexican food, but I got hooked on smothered burritos and guacamole, which were always good with beer.

When next May came around, the job was finishing up and my father was calling me to come back and help him build a slaughterhouse about forty miles outside St. Louis, just north of Winfield, Missouri. He finally convinced me—even though by this time I liked Colorado and had no intentions of ever moving back to Illinois. I loved Denver's sunshine, weather, and mountains.

My father signed a union agreement with the bricklayers and laborers out of St. Louis saying he would use their union labor on the slaughterhouse project. He brought over a few union bricklayers from Illinois to help, but the St. Louis union didn't want outsiders in their backyard. The union bylaws in St. Louis called for two men to pick up an eight-inch concrete block to lay it in the wall. The block weighs thirty-eight pounds

RANDOM TANGENTS

and I was laying them one handed like my father did with no problem. The block layers from St. Louis would show up with their house slippers on and were so slow you had to hang a plumb bob from their nose to see if they moved. My father had bid the job with a production rate of 400 blocks laid per day per block layer. The St. Louis guys couldn't lay 400 blocks between four of them and they were trying to make a point to an out-of-state contractor.

My father ran them off and told them they were feather bedding his job. I started laying the blocks myself when three of these union guys showed up. One was the business agent for the bricklayers, one a business agent for the laborers and the third guy was about six feet six weighing between 275 to 300 pounds and looked like a typical thug. I heard he worked for the mob out of St. Louis. As they watched me lay blocks, they were telling me what I could and couldn't do. Finally, I crawled out of the footing with my masonry trowel. I was ready to open that guy up from top to bottom if they didn't leave. They got the hint and left while knowing they had made their point.

We found out that the attorney for the union was the brother of the guy we were building the slaughterhouse for. The attorney called his brother and said to get it ironed out pronto as there was going to be a contract put out to take care of the contractor. When I heard that, I went ballistic! I told them I could just watch over the property and set up some booby traps to catch them coming in. The owner told us to just settle it and he would pay the difference. The owner and his brother told me if the mob caught me driving down the road in that little black MGB, they would run me off the road or shoot me. The slaughterhouse wasn't worth fighting over so father had the union guys come back to work; they slowed down production. I was

THE AMERICAN DREAM

mixing mortar for them to lay the blocks with and they would just shovel it down the holes in the block without laying any. After that experience I had a bad taste for unions in St. Louis. These workers weren't doing an honest day's work for an honest day's pay (as the unions liked to preach).

While building the project, I would head back to Illinois some weekends to see my mother and visit old friends. One Saturday, I walked into the little bank in town and ran into a young lady working there who I had never seen before. She was a very attractive farm girl named Jan and we soon started dating. She was working at the bank during the summer and getting ready to finish her last year in college to become a teacher. As she headed back to school the job in Missouri was winding up so I headed back to Colorado in a new blue MGB that I had just traded my old one for. I started working that summer on a new warehouse building for Gerald H. Phipps Construction. When winter hit that year, the job froze up and didn't thaw out until the following March. In the meantime, I found a job in North Denver where they made Chaparral snowmobiles. I worked in the metal treatment area where they treated the metal runners for the snowmobiles with chemicals before the runners were painted. We were also treating metal rocket blades that were used on rockets fired from gunships in Vietnam. It seemed like everyone got a piece of the action from the war.

By this time, my father and mother had sold their house in Illinois and moved to Florida. I thought Florida would be a good place to spend the winter so off I went. My father vouched for me and got me into the Orlando union hall for bricklayers and cement masons. My father had been working as a stone mason while they were building Disney World and laid the

RANDOM TANGENTS

stone for Tom Sawyer's Island and the Japanese pearl diving pool. I was working on the new Sea World that was under construction until the temperatures warmed up back in Colorado. It was late March 1973; the warehouse project was starting up again, so it was time for me to go. During this time, I had been staying in touch with Jan back in Illinois. She had moved to Chicago and was teaching at a school there, so I made a detour on my way back to see her. It didn't go as I had hoped; a boyfriend left flowers on her doorstep the same night I was there.

When I got back to Colorado, I knew that nice little MGB was going to get torn up driving out to the construction site. I sold it. I bought an old 1958 Chevrolet and put some covers over the seats to spruce it up. I also had to put a couple of pieces of plywood under the floor mats as the floor was rusting out—a typical '58 Chevy. I didn't mind as cars were just a means of transportation and this one would keep me out of trouble!

By the end of that project, I was starting to be known in the company. Over the next two years, I moved up and became the concrete superintendent. I worked hard in scheduling crews on the numerous projects and ensured quality work. At that time, we were building hospitals, parking structures, banks, medical offices, and industrial buildings.

At night I would go to the bar with the crew, drink beer, and smoke Lucky Strike cigarettes as my grandfather once did. One Saturday morning I woke up and started thinking about what I was doing in life and where I was heading. The drinking and smoking weren't getting me anywhere, so I quit drinking with the guys every night and eventually quit smoking. I wanted a clear head and a direction in my life instead of being in a stupor night after night.

THE AMERICAN DREAM

I wasn't the first in the family to do so. The morning he turned sixty-five, my grandfather went out the back door of his house to throw out his Lucky Strike cigarette butts onto the ground as he had always done. He started counting all of the butts on the ground. He quit that day after having smoked for the better part of his life. A few years later he was diagnosed with throat cancer and they had to take out his voice box. He learned how to speak with a vibrator next to his throat and how he could compress air in his lungs and force it out so he could somehow talk. He was as tough as shoe leather.

I remember stopping by to see him. In the winter he would make what he called "cookies," which were actually thick fudge brownies, and would offer you some along with a cup of coffee. When he made coffee, he would add some grounds to the coffee pot and heat the water until it boiled. Once the pot had too many grounds in it, he would dump them out and start over. As soon as he could get back into his garden in the spring, he was out there from sunup until sundown—planting and weeding his garden. He sold vegetables, strawberries, and blackberries to anyone who wanted them. He didn't do it to make money but to visit with people. I enjoyed the time I spent with him.

Jan got back in touch with me that fall and said she wanted to see me again. I thought about it for a couple of days, then called her back and told her there was only one way I was coming back to see her and that was to make it permanent. I bought an engagement ring and headed back to Illinois around Christmas time.

Getting married in the Catholic church wasn't an easy deal as I had to take some classes and talk with the priest in charge. Well, this priest, being an old guy, told me if I didn't convert and become a Catholic, I would go to hell. I was about ready to tell him I would see him there but bit my tongue.

At the wedding, which took place in this little country church out in the middle of farming country, everyone was seated and waiting for it to start and all we were missing was the priest. A mad rush was on to find him, and they finally managed to contact him as he was having dinner with a church official. Either he was just cantankerous or had a real bad memory problem. (But if he couldn't remember this, how was he supposed to find his way to heaven?)

The day after the wedding, July 4, 1976, we moved to Loveland, Colorado, where my wife started school in Ft. Collins. She graduated with her master's degree two years later. Shortly after we were married, I decided to start a business and asked my brother if he wanted to be part of it. We started a concrete placing and finishing company. I went to the office of Gerald H. Phipps Construction and told them what I wanted to do, and they offered their support and gave me all their concrete work if I maintained quality and at a fair price.

We started with approximately $30,000 in the bank and were signatory to the cement masons and laborers union. I sold two lots I had on a spring-fed canal that ran out to the ocean in Florida to raise some money, while my brother took a loan from his in-laws. Our first project was for 250,000 square feet of concrete placement on an IBM building in Niwot, Colorado. We were paid like clockwork every thirty days. I quickly understood why all the subcontractors in Denver wanted to work for Gerald H. Phipps Construction.

After two years the business was doing well, and I was thinking about what I thought married life was supposed to be like. I just imagined that once in a while I should get a kiss or

THE AMERICAN DREAM

hug when coming in the door or some kind of acknowledgement; it seemed something was amiss. One Saturday morning when I came back from the gas station I started a conversation that would change all my thoughts about where I was and where I was going.

"Jan, in two years of marriage not once have you ever given me a hug or kiss when I come home, and you don't tell me that you love me. Is there something wrong?"

"I will try to learn to love you."

"If you don't love me, then why did you marry me?"

"Well, all my friends were getting married."

The conversation was short and to the point. Not one that I was expecting. That was like driving a wooden stake in my heart. I walked out the front door and went walking for four or five hours up the Big Thompson River almost to the foot of the mountains. I had been completely disillusioned about love and marriage. I thought my wife loved me and the hurt I felt at this point ultimately led to some drastic decisions. I don't like giving up and decided to try and go forward to make this marriage work. I was thirty years old; I wanted to start having children and a family. I didn't want to destroy that possibility.

After graduating from college my wife started looking for a job and I asked her to possibly find one close to Denver so that I didn't have to drive 120 miles round trip every day for work. In the end she accepted an offer close to where we were. I asked her about moving to Denver and for her to commute as I was putting in a lot of hours. She was willing to move halfway in between but would not move to Denver, so we stayed where we were.

Toward the end of her first year of teaching she became pregnant and we moved to Denver to start raising our family.

RANDOM TANGENTS

We first welcomed a son and then a daughter two years later—right after we bought a house in Littleton, Colorado. The children made life worth living and I worked hard to make money to buy the house and refurbish it.

As time went on, I hustled more work from some of the larger contractors in town, and we were running up to sixty men full time when we were busiest. We ended up buying our own concrete pumping equipment and had our own shop and office. We were doing well until 1983, when the oil shale boom died in Colorado and the money dried up overnight. Oil companies left town and there were vacant office buildings everywhere in downtown Denver. On some of the projects, the developers just turned the lights off and left buildings without them being completed. Denver had always been a boom-or-bust town and now we were in a definite bust cycle. The competition was so fierce for the available work that contractors and subcontractors were doing it on a breakeven basis or less, just trying to survive.

During those seven years in business with our team, we were covering two, sometimes three, projects a day. One project, which was a parking garage in downtown Denver, will always stick in my memory. Before we started the project, I had gone by and talked to the superintendent in charge of it. I was concerned about the high-voltage lines that ran down the alley next to where the new parking structure was going to be built. I asked if he was going to cover the lines with insulation or bury them underground. He said he would talk to the power company about it. As construction began, I asked again about the power lines and he said that the power company was not going to cover them as they were ten feet from the building,

THE AMERICAN DREAM

and he wasn't going to bury them either. It truly worried me that my crew was going to be working near those power lines.

One morning we were placing concrete on the fourth floor, about level with the high-power electric lines, when my fears came true. Our plan was to start placing concrete along the edge closest to the power lines and work away from them, making sure we didn't get the long handles connected to our floats into contact with them. I left that project and went over to another one we were working on. About two hours later, I received a phone call that one of our guys had hit the power line and had fallen four floors to the alley below. I rushed to the hospital only to find out he didn't make it. I had to face his wife and family. Days like that are extremely tough and one questions oneself about the risk of being in business and taking the responsibility for others.

When his wife asked me what killed her husband, I told her it was the fall and not the electrical shock. What I learned later was that he had gone back to the side where we had started placing concrete. He was going to fix a little discrepancy in the floor with a float that had a long handle on it. As he pushed the float out and drew it back to him, the aluminum handles hit the high-voltage lines, and he was launched off the edge of the building to the alley below and landed on his back. The subcontractor, being in a rush, had left a one-foot opening in the handrail exactly where he hit the high-voltage lines, allowing our worker to fall to the alley below. The impact of the fall tore the aorta out of his heart, and he bled to death internally. There was nothing anyone could do.

This was a tragedy for our company and for all the guys who worked for us—we were a team of brothers. This fellow was an ordained minister, and he and his wife had decided to

RANDOM TANGENTS

move up to Denver from Colorado Springs so he could be part of our team. He was one of the best, and his death was a big loss. One never gets over things like this. Life goes on, but there is always that memory.

Later, it was found out that the superintendent on the project had the funds to bury or insulate the lines but decided against doing either so as to save money for his bonus pool. I will never underestimate safety to save a few dollars; unfortunately, not all of us think the same way.

As I said, 1983 was not a good year for construction and we were struggling to procure work as we were getting beat by 40 percent on our bids by nonunion operations. The union contracts were expiring, and the unions wanted a raise for their people. I brought together three of the larger subcontractors in Denver that controlled approximately 35 percent of the membership in the cement masons' union. We were going to negotiate with the union as one entity in hopes that this would give us a little more bargaining power. First, we didn't want to go nonunion as we wished to keep paying into the benefits package so that our employees had insurance and retirement. Negotiations went on for two months and came to a point where we finally had to go nonunion as we couldn't be competitive any longer.

During the union strike of 1983 I had friends who were carpenters come over to our house and help me remodel it as I worked on the landscaping and painting. It was really starting to look like something and one day when I had just finished some landscaping I asked my wife why she hadn't said one word about how nice it looked. Her response was that she had told the neighbors how nice it looked. That was about the final straw in our relationship.

THE AMERICAN DREAM

Prior to that, even after seeking marriage counseling, the marriage had continued to crumble. I was discovering my need to be wanted and cared for and the turmoil blew apart the remaining fragments of the marriage. The turmoil was threatening my ability to take care of my business.

My wife by this time had taken some more college courses and started teaching again. At the end of her first year of teaching she gained her tenure so that she was assured of a job going forward. At this time, I knew it was time to call an end to the marriage.

One day my wife asked why I even came home, and I told her there were only two reasons that I came home, and they were standing next to her. I loved them with all my heart.

As time went on, I moved out, rented an apartment, and furnished it so that my children could stay with me. They stayed a lot with me that summer of 1983. We went up to Glenwood Springs by train and went swimming at the big hot springs pool there for several days. We drove around in the old 1959 Corvette I had with a tape deck. We would play the *American Graffiti* tape with all the old tunes and sing together. We knew them all by heart. We had a great time being together that summer.

Here I was, trying to survive in business amid economic downturn, negotiating with the unions, and in the middle of a divorce. The sky seemed to be falling. What would be the next direction to take?

I was able to sell my business share to my brother and took up scuba diving while going through my divorce, which seemed to be dragging on forever. Once the children were back in school, I grabbed my scuba diving gear and off I went to visit parts of the world I had never seen.

CHAPTER SEVEN
Cutting Loose: Truk Lagoon

It was 1983 when I decided to take some time and go scuba diving across the Pacific. With the help of a travel agent who knew the region well, I bought a one-way ticket to the island of Truk to go diving and a one-way ticket from Hong Kong back to the U.S. It was up to me to decide what to do in between; I had two months to explore.

I packed my dive bag and gear along with a few clothes and off I went. Since I didn't receive my R&R while in Vietnam but saw pictures and heard stories from the guys coming back from Bangkok, Kuala Lumpur, and Singapore, I decided it was time to explore that part of the world. I had recently purchased a small scuba diving book that detailed a lot of the dive spots and shops across the Pacific, so I had some ideas about where to go. My travel agent had given me brochures of the touristy places and filled me in on things to do while in Hong Kong. I was looking forward to this vacation as a reprieve from the seven years of hard work I had put into building a construction business. I was ready for my R&R.

I flew across the ocean, stopping at a couple of U.S. islands before finally arriving at Truk island. It had a landing strip, a small mountainous hill, and a lagoon called Truk Lagoon (for

CUTTING LOOSE: TRUK LAGOON

obvious reasons). During World War II, the Japanese had a base on the island and hid many of their ships in the lagoon. The U.S. had been actively looking for the Japanese fleet. Once an American plane spotted them, the ensuing attack lasted for three days, destroying over 200 planes and sinking over forty ships. In only three days, it became the largest sunken ship graveyard in the world.

The lagoon had a white sand bottom and a depth of over 200 feet. There were several ships that you could scuba dive on within thirty to 120 feet of the surface. At that time, they didn't have nitrox, rebreathers, or helium mixed gas available on the island, so it was strictly sport diving with regular air. You always had to be vigilant of the time you were down, the depth, and the amount of air you had left in your tank. Today they have rebreathers, diving computers, and much more sophisticated diving gear. Back then we only had a depth gauge for the depth we were diving, a tank pressure gauge letting us know how much air we had left, and a watch to tell us how much time we had left to spend underwater before it was time to surface.

My dive buddy while I was in Truk was an F-16 pilot and instructor. He was a short guy, and I teased him about having to sit on a telephone book in order to see out of his cockpit. "I might be short, but that just means I can take more g-force than you since my heart is closer to my brain!" he shot back. He could get into places I couldn't. He went inside the bridge on one of the sunken ships and came out with a skull to show me before putting it back where he found it. We went diving on six different ships while I was there, all loaded with torpedoes, trucks, planes, tanks, and ammunition.

We were diving with the Blue Lagoon Dive Shop owned by Kimiuo Aisek. He was just seventeen years old when the

RANDOM TANGENTS

Americans attacked the Japanese at Truk in 1944. His knowledge of the sunken vessels in the lagoon and the history was unparalleled. Kimiuo had a recompression chamber (that only he knew how to operate) on the island in case a diver got the bends from being underwater at depth for too long. He also had it there in case of an emergency when he was diving deep recovering human remains.

His dive shop had small plywood boats that could take four divers out at a time into the lagoon. The young boys who navigated these small boats were amazing to watch. They would stop over a sunken ship and throw a line over with a brick tied to it as an anchor and tell us to dive to the ship below. I couldn't see anything, but these young boys had so frequented the diving spots that they knew exactly where the sunken ships were by triangulating the distance from the surrounding land, hills, and reef.

Kimiuo and I became pretty good friends over the course of the week I was there. He talked about how he had dived most of the ships that were sunk and recovered the remains off them for the Japanese, who would come once a year for a ceremony commemorating the attack. Kimiuo would give them whatever remains he had found. Kimiuo asked me to stay and help him run his dive shop, which was an enticing offer. The catch was that I would have had to marry a Trukese lady. I liked Kimiuo, but I had places to go and things to see. Frankly, I didn't want to be stuck on an island out in the middle of the Pacific.

The plane I had flown into Truk on had only a few seats, as the back of the plane was used for hauling cargo and supplies to the islands. At that time, it was only landing on the island twice a week and the Trukese would come and watch it land and take off. It was a highlight of their week watching the landing and takeoff of these planes, so I got a proper farewell when I was leaving. No popcorn or milkshake stands for this entertainment!

Palau

Next stop was Palau. Even though I wanted to be free to go anywhere, when I arrived in Truk the customs officer stamping my passport asked to see my return ticket. I had to explain that I was planning on buying one in Truk to my next destination. That didn't go over too well as the officer didn't want me to be stuck on their island. Eventually, I had to go over to the travel agent down the street and book onward tickets to Palau and then to Jakarta.

Palau was the perfect spot to do some more diving in an area that was also a battleground during World War II. Even though I traveled by myself, I was always able to find some dive partners who had the same interests. In Palau, I met a couple from Richardson, Texas—Ray and Beth—and another couple who were on their honeymoon. We dove together for most of the five days I was there.

Another fellow joined us for a couple of days, but he wasn't a happy sort. One morning when it was raining, we put our dive gear in the back of an open truck and climbed in for the ride to our dive boat. It was a warm tropical rain, but this guy constantly complained about getting wet. The young lady of the newlywed couple spouted off and told him, "You aren't a sugar tit, so you're not going to melt. Just shut up!" I almost fell out of that truck laughing! That was the last day he went diving with us!

RANDOM TANGENTS

The day I arrived, I ran into an American walking around the island who was under house arrest. He said the island's shore patrol had come aboard his sailboat before he came into the harbor and found his rifle. He said he had it onboard for protection as some of the islands around the Philippines were known to have pirates. Sailing solo in this part of the world could be dangerous if you didn't know the places to stay away from. However, having rifles was against the law in Palau so they motored his boat into the small marina and pulled the prop off so he couldn't escape. He had to sleep in their jail at night but could walk around the island during the day as he couldn't really flee.

One day between dives we went ashore on a small island for our lunch break. The dive master climbed a palm tree and knocked down some coconuts and opened them up for us so we could drink the coconut water. Then he took a net and went out into the water and brought back fresh sardines. We were playing real islanders—eating raw sardines and drinking coconut water. It was great until the next day when the bacteria in the uncooked seafood would catch up with you.

Another day, we went by boat over to another island called Peleliu, which was a major battleground towards the end of World War II. The Japanese controlled the runway there and were well fortified to protect it. The U.S. lost a lot of men taking this island, but it was deemed necessary for the U.S. to control. It would provide the Army with a runway and a base to operate from on the march across the Pacific to free the islands Japan had taken. The runway was still there, along with some old artillery pieces. Not much of a memorial for all the men that lost their lives there. How many people even remember it today?

One of the last dives we did in Palau was on another sunken ship that was ninety feet down to the top deck. The young guy running the boat dropped the anchor (brick) overboard onto the ship and we went down to explore. While we were down there, the brick slipped off the deck of the ship. With nothing holding the small boat in place anymore, it drifted about a quarter mile away by the time we got to the surface. After a little shouting, he finally woke up to the noise we were making or else it would have been a long swim back to shore!

While in Palau, Ray, Beth, and I went out to dinner one evening to sample some of the local cuisine. We started talking to the locals and noticed an old guy chewing a large bean wrapped in a leaf and spitting black stuff in a can on the floor. They said it was betel nut. You put it in your mouth, chewed on it, and the spat out the saliva that had turned black. In time it turned all their teeth black. I had witnessed this in Vietnam with the Montagnard tribes that sometimes worked for us in the Central Highlands. The older women of the tribe would have black teeth from chewing the betel nut as it gave them sort of a buzz. The younger girls had white teeth as they were more into smoking marijuana. By the end of the week in Palau, Ray, Beth, and I became pretty good friends as they loved to have fun and a few drinks in the evening. We promised to stay in touch once we got back to the States. We would meet up again.

Indonesia

My next stop was Jakarta, where I was supposed to stay one night before catching a plane up to North Sulawesi to a town called Manado. I had read in my little diving adventure book

RANDOM TANGENTS

that there was some good diving there, even though it was off the beaten track. I was feeling adventurous.

As I flew into Jakarta, I looked out the plane's window and saw this green band of water that extended out from the city a couple of miles or so. In time I figured it out that it was a polluted band of water that you didn't want to be in. I found out that the Dutch had dug sanitation canals around the city back in the late 1500s and early 1600s. It was one of the most modern cities back then. However, with the growth of the city, the canals turned into no more than stagnant ponds full of waste.

We landed at the international airport, and from there I caught a taxi to a room I had booked. On the way to the hotel, the traffic, with all the tuk-tuks running around, combined with the heavy smell of waste, made me a little nauseated and I was glad I was only staying there for one night.

When I checked in at the hotel, I decided to go out for a drink at a local bar so I asked the doorman where I should go. He said to go to the "Hot Men Bar." The name sounded funny, so I asked again, and he told me the same thing. He signaled a taxi for me and told the taxi driver where to take me. Soon, we were driving up a dead-end alley off a side street and I was getting a little bit uncomfortable.

Finally, the taxi driver pointed to a neon sign hanging over a door at the end of the alley. There it was. Hot Men Bar. I paid him and went into the bar, wondering what the hell I was doing here? I sat down at the bar and ordered a beer. The next thing I knew, a young lady came up and wanted to get friendly. I told her I was there just for a beer and maybe some dancing. As soon as she turned away, another came up to me and it was the same story. This went on for three or four girls before they finally left me alone.

CUTTING LOOSE: TRUK LAGOON

Fortunately, I managed to make it back to my hotel in one piece. The next morning was a rush as I had to catch a plane up to Manado. I jumped into a taxi in front of the hotel and asked to be taken to the airport. When I arrived, I rushed inside only to find out that they had two airports—one international and one domestic. I was at the international airport and by the time I got to the domestic, the plane had taken off. Now I had to spend another glorious night in sweet-smelling, insanely humid Jakarta.

I found a little hotel not far from the domestic terminal and called it an early night. By this time, I wanted out of there! I got to the domestic terminal in plenty of time the next morning and boarded the Air Garuda jet. While we were taxiing down the runway and picking up speed for takeoff, the front door going into the cockpit was open. I was wondering if we were going to make it off the runway as it looked like a couple of drunks were driving this plane. We were weaving back and forth. Finally, we took off, and I could at least relax until we had to land. Later, I found out that Air Garuda didn't have the best safety record as an airline.

The stewardesses started serving lunch once we got into the air. The lunch was in prepackaged, white cardboard boxes with grease leeching through the sides. No, thanks, ma'am, I am not hungry! Once we "safely" landed, we deplaned down the steps and into the 20x20 terminal building. As the baggage was being brought in, I noticed that I was the only English-speaking person there and began wondering how I was going to get to the hotel.

When I picked up my dive bag, a young man came over and pointed at a dive poster on the wall. I nodded yes. I showed him the name and address of my hotel that I had on a piece of paper, and he motioned for me to follow him. He had a taxi and took me to the hotel. Luckily, the receptionist spoke a little English, so I could converse with the taxi driver through her. He agreed to come back the next morning to take me to the dive shop that had accommodations along with diving. It was all working out! The next morning we went around the bay to an undeveloped area where the dive shop was. The fellow who owned it, Loky Herlambang, spoke fluent English and French besides Indonesian. The accommodations were grass-thatched huts with an outdoor shower. Food was served family-style, so everyone got to know each other. The price, which included two dives, accommodations, and food was $60 per day. The dive boats were large hollowed-out logs with storage in the bottom for your scuba tanks. There was a small outboard motor on the back and outriggers on the sides that stabilized it as it sliced through the water.

 The young guys and girls who took you diving were all certified scuba divemasters who Loky had trained. They were conscientious and tried to make sure you had a good diving experience. They all loved the water and working with guests. I would remember this later when I set up my own diving operation. Smiles and being attentive mean everything!

 When we went diving, there was a wall that we dived on and the fish and coral were beautiful. The only drawback was that when it rained, the polluted water would flow out of the canals into the bay. It never seemed to quite reach the wall we dived on, but I was there for only a short time. Loky told me that he had a glass-bottomed boat and took officials out on it to show them the rich marine life and the coral to get them to turn the area into a marine park. He said they were going to approve the conservation effort, thus saving the area for future generations and to promote diving and tourism.

Loky and I quickly became friends. I told him about some of the places I had been diving and about the shipwrecks. He asked me if I wanted to dive on a wreck in about 120 feet of water. He said he didn't normally take anyone down to it because of the depth. We went down and had a look at the hull of the ship. As we swam around it, you could see that it had buckled in the middle. It must have hit the reef, which ruptured the outer skin, after which it sank quickly. The ship must have been traveling at a fair speed and had a weak structure to have buckled like it did.

I enjoyed my time there with the simplicity of the operation and the friendliness of everyone at the dive shop. They lived day to day as life went by and stress didn't seem to be in their vocabulary. We shared meals together and they were always laughing about something.

Bali

It was time for my next stop: Bali. Even though it is not a diving spot, I had heard about how great a place it was, so I decided to stop there. In 1983 it was quickly becoming developed by the tourist industry with nice hotels, restaurants, and night clubs. They had a nice beach you could enjoy with vendors coming around with their hibachi, wishing to cook some satay for you with peanut sauce. Oh, yes, and there was beer to follow!

Bali was a wonderful destination with many things to see such as the famous wood carvings, batik design clothes, different temples, and elaborate funeral parades. I went to the Goa Gajah, or elephant cave, which is a meditation cave surrounded with rock carvings. Hinduism was the primary religion here, and the temples seemed to blend into the countryside. The funeral parades are also unique on the island as they are more like big festivals.

I saw a dive shop and asked where the best diving was. It seemed it was on the other side of the island and they weren't all that enthused to take only one person over there for the day. I finally talked them into it with the help of a little money, and we set off the next morning. When we arrived, they pointed out into the bay close to a rock sticking up and said that was the dive site. It seemed I was going to be diving alone again, which is a big no-no, but I decided I would do it and stay within fifteen meters (fifty feet) of the surface so that my air would last for a while. The dive turned out to be okay with a large school of barracuda that surrounded me as I went down, and we all swam together for quite some time.

On the way back, we stopped at a monkey sanctuary where you could walk out into the trees that were filled with monkeys making all kinds of noise. There were vendors who sold popcorn so you could feed the monkeys. It was just another tourist thing.

I met an English fellow on my flight from Manado to Bali and we happened to stay at the same hotel on Bali. We decided to go out and have a few beers, so we went to a night club where there was some dancing. We were having a good time, but soon he left with a beautiful young lady in a white dress. The following morning, I noticed her leaving the hotel and the security guards at the hotel were giving her a bad time and told her not to come back.

Two nights later, just before I left, we met down at the pool to have a few drinks at the bar. We met a couple of Australian ladies there who were also leaving the next day, and we had a raging good time. One of the Australian girls, Barb, even gave me her contact information in case I ever made it to Melbourne.

Malaysia

Leaving Bali, I flew to Singapore. After clearing customs, I was walking through the terminal and saw a flight departure sign for a plane leaving for Kuala Lumpur in one hour. I decided that was a place to go, so I bought a ticket and jumped on the plane. I knew I could catch Singapore later.

Kuala Lumpur had noticeably changed since the Vietnam war. There were no GIs coming here for R&R, therefore no red-light districts full of girls and bars waiting for the soldiers, at least not to my knowledge. I spent a couple of days touring around the booming city. I could see that a lot of Korean and Japanese money was pouring in as high-rises and manufacturing facilities were proliferating. Seems that manufacturing clothes and certain goods from Malaysia and then exporting them directly to the U.S. was profitable. The companies realized that starting up there meant cheap labor. This was a time where international business and finding the right investments by using international export laws was in favor.

I stopped and talked to the young man working at the front desk of the hotel. He asked me if I would like to join him and his wife for dinner at an outside café. We met later that evening and had a nice Malaysian-style dinner. They had a lot of questions about America and I enjoyed answering them. I went to pay for the check, and they said they would prefer to pay as they were pleased to be in my company. I knew that he didn't make that much money working at the hotel. I was humbled by their gesture.

I asked the concierge at the hotel where I could go diving in Malaysia and was told there was a little island off the east coast called Pulau Tioman. The following day I caught a small two-engine prop plane at the domestic terminal. Before we landed on the small airstrip, we buzzed it to clear the cattle away. After landing the ride to the hotel was a four-wheel drive Toyota truck with an open back with seating. I threw in my dive gear and clothes, and we headed to the only hotel on the island. The asphalt road only lasted for about one hundred feet once we left the terminal, then we were on dirt roads.

Upon arriving at the hotel, which was more like a motel, I checked in to a small room with running water and a shower. That's all I needed so everything was good. I noticed an arrow on the ceiling and figured it must be the direction of Mecca for the Muslim clients. I went to dinner that evening and met an English couple that were vacationing there. The guy's name was Chibi, and he was a commercial hardhat diver working on oil rigs in the North Sea. His girlfriend, Sheila, had flown in from England to be with him for a holiday. We talked about diving, of course, and planned to go scuba diving the next day to check things out.

The next day the weather was beautiful as we went over to the small dive shop. We asked to rent some tanks and weight belts. They rented us the gear without even looking at our diving certifications and took us out on a small boat. I thought it was funny they didn't check us out as they were supposedly a *Professional Association of Diving Instructors* (PADI)-certified dive shop. We did a couple of dives, but they were disappointing. I think the islanders had used pipe bombs or dynamite on the reef to get the fish, so the coral was pretty broken up and dead. It also had a lot of algae growing on it from the excess nutrients in the water or pollution (raw sewage).

The next day I went swimming to a small island some distance out from the beach. I had my fins and mask on, but I didn't think much about swimming that far out until I got to the island. There seemed to be quite a few sharks swimming around it, so I decided to swim back to shore quickly. Probably nothing to worry about, but I looked like the only meal around.

That night, Chibi, Sheila, and I found a small shop along the beach that served fish and rice. They cooked the fresh fish outside on their charcoal grill. The total cost for the meal and drink was only $2.

Singapore

Chibi and Sheila were flying to Singapore the next day, so I tagged along as we were having a lot of fun together, drinking beer and telling stories. He had some exciting stories about diving in the North Sea for the offshore oil companies down to depths of 800 feet. Of course, they used mixed gas and had decompression chambers on the ships for the divers. The time in the chamber is made as comfortable as possible as they gradually lower the pressure to decompress you. The chambers even had cots so you could sleep.

He said it was dangerous work, but the pay was pretty good. I asked about the possibility of long-term effects that deep diving would have on a human body. Chibi said that nobody really knew. In the end, was the risk worth the reward?

We decided to meet up at an outside café area called Bugis Street in an old part of Singapore one evening. They had been there before and said this was the place where things were happening. We sat at a sidewalk café and ordered fresh live crab boiled in a chili broth. Of course, we had plenty of beer in one-liter bottles to keep us hydrated.

As the night progressed, the streets were shut down and tables were set up. About 2:00 a.m. the bars and night clubs closed, and everyone came to Bugis Street. You could sit, eat, drink, and watch the crazies until daylight. Now things were starting to get interesting! The street hawkers were walking up and down the street to every table trying to sell their trinkets. Back then, the movie *E.T.* had come out and the street hawkers had E.T. dolls with a blinking light on the finger you could point at anyone and laugh. I bought one just for fun as we were getting a little tipsy by this time!

A group of eight Aussies took one of the tables in the middle of the street and were seriously knocking back some beer and having a great time. Some "girls" showed up from the clubs and started walking down the street when suddenly one of the Aussie guys pulled a girl onto his lap. All I heard was a scream, and soon all the Aussies were laughing their bum off. The police quickly came over to the Aussies' table to see what was going on, so they calmed down for a few minutes.

I was quick to learn that these dressed-up ladies were called lady-boys. What an experience that was to see! Some of them were dressed to the max and had bodies that looked just like girls except for the Adam's apple that was prevalent on some. I came to find out that this area was where all the transvestites and transsexuals hung out at night after the clubs closed.

We continued to drink and watch people until the sun was coming up and decided to call it a night—or morning, whatever. What an experience! Years later, Bugis Street was cleaned up and turned into a mecca for shoppers and bargain hunters. The colorful and seedy nightlife of Bugis Street is history.

There were a few things I wanted to see in Singapore, and one was the historic Raffles Hotel. They had an afternoon tea that you could enjoy with piano and violin playing, which brought back nostalgic moments. The hotel was in need of renovation, and it was rumored that they were going to rebuild it to its grand excellence of fifty years prior. Of course, I had to try a Singapore sling at the Long Bar in the Raffles Hotel, as this is where it had been originally concocted. I was never much of a gin drinker and a couple of these would knock you back.

Thailand

Singapore was a lot of fun and I had enjoyed spending time with the English couple, but soon I was boarding a plane for Phuket, Thailand. Upon landing, Thai customs gave me a two-week tourist visa, more than I thought I needed. I also planned to go to Rangoon in Burma and see the Shwedagon Golden Pagoda, which was built 2,500 years ago. I had acquired the necessary visa, so it was on my list after Thailand and before going to Hong Kong.

Phuket was not really a scuba diving destination; I was there to enjoy the beach and tour the island. The best scuba diving, I was told, was at the Similan Islands, which were reachable by a live aboard boat trip that lasted several days. I didn't have the time! I tried one dive in Phuket, but everything was covered in algae and the coral was dead, so I didn't stay down long. As the guy helped me back into the boat with my gear, he asked if I had seen the big eel down there. He said the eel had taken a man's leg off the week before. Now he tells me!

RANDOM TANGENTS

While there, I enjoyed the night life and the beach. It was laid back with the sound of the ocean lapping the shore. How could you leave this? But all things come to an end, and it was time to go and chase the rest of the adventure. Next stop, Bangkok.

I had booked a room at the luxurious Grand Hyatt Bangkok. After I checked in, I heard a knock on the door, and a plate of fresh fruit and a teapot were brought into my room. I just needed to figure out how to get around Bangkok. I went to the concierge and asked about renting a car and he said the hotel had automobiles with a driver for $8 per hour. I thought this was a great way to get around the city, so I was off.

My driver and I started to talk, and soon it turned out that he had been a soldier in the Black Panther Division of Thailand and served in Vietnam. We had something in common and it gave us a connection. He said when he got out of the Thai Army he took up Thai kickboxing full time. As we drove, he pointed out the arena where kickboxing matches were held during the week. He said that he made it to the top but quit as most of the money he was fighting for was going to the promoter. Kickboxing is a national sport in Thailand, and you can see young guys practicing it about anywhere you go.

He asked where I wanted to go, and I suggested the Grand Palace. I was glad he was driving as the traffic was crazy, even more tuk-tuks than in Jakarta, and I didn't have a clue where anything was. We arrived at the Grand Palace and went onto the grounds after paying the entrance fee. It was amazing. We spent half the day there. The highlight was the Temple of the Emerald Buddha, located on the Palace's grounds. The spectacular temple was covered in gold leaf. To go in, one must take their shoes off and leave them in a rack. Once inside, it is best

CUTTING LOOSE: TRUK LAGOON

to revere the worshippers who are seated on the floor, praying and meditating. The Emerald Buddha is a small statue made from jade or jasper and only stands about twenty-six inches tall. The Emerald Buddha had a scarf draped across its shoulder. Depending on the time of year, the color of the scarf would be different.

The next temple we saw was that of the Reclining Buddha, which is one of the oldest temples in Thailand. It is a large, long building, and once inside, you see the Reclining Buddha, which is approximately 150 feet long and about forty-five feet high at the head. It was made from brick and mortar in the sixteenth century. People coming to see the Reclining Buddha could put a donation in a box and were given a little square of gold leaf that they could attach to the statue. Over the years, as the little pieces of gold leaf build up, it would be coated with lacquer to help maintain a glossy golden finish.

The driver and I were getting along quite well, and he asked if I wanted to get something to drink. I was all in as it was getting to be late afternoon and was a fairly warm day. We drove to a building that had a small bar, and he motioned me into a large room where girls were sitting behind a glass wall. He said I could choose one if I wished. Gee whiz and wow! Later, I asked if any of these lovely young ladies happened to speak English, and he said that the three sitting on the bottom bench did. One of them was really cute, and she had the number 007 on her lapel, which made me laugh. Since we were in a so-called "massage parlor," I asked what the price was for a full-body massage. He said only $100, which included everything!

You are probably wondering what a full-body massage is. These girls escort you to a private room, where you take your clothes off so they can give you a rinse under a shower. The shower in this room was tiled and large. On the floor was an air mattress and you were told to lie face down on it while she took a large plastic tub and made up a batch of soapy water with a lot of bubbles that she poured onto your body. Next, she lay on you and started moving all over your backside, scrubbing your body with her body. Then she moved underneath of you and sort of did the same thing. After that, she had you stand up as she rinsed you off then asked what else you wished to do. There was a big round bed in the room as well. End of story.

    I had asked her why she was working here. She told me she was from Chiang Mai and came down here to make money to send back to her family as was common practice. I had heard that the most beautiful ladies in Thailand came from northern Thailand around Chiang Mai. They have a totally different culture, value system and value of life in Thailand, and you must appreciate that as you are in their country.

    I had heard about massage parlors from the guys coming back from R&R while I was in Vietnam, and now I was here. It seemed the GIs would fly in and end up at one of these places and pick a girl they wanted to spend a week with. If they liked her, they kept her and if not, they traded her off for another one. That seemed kind of cold hearted. They said the best thing to do was give them your money and let them negotiate costs for you at all the places you went. During the war, it must have helped the economy of Bangkok, Kuala Lumpur, Taipei, Singapore, and a few other places.

    My driver and I didn't get back to the hotel until after midnight and I was tuckered out. Next day around noon we partnered up again, and as soon as we got out of the driveway of the hotel, he stopped and took his chauffeur's hat off, and I jumped into the front seat. We were going out for another adventurous day!

We were going to see the Jim Thompson House, which was now a museum. Jim Thompson was an OSS operative at the end of World War II, and he decided there was a lot of opportunity in Thailand, so he made it his home. At that time, the country was in a poor economic state and he saw an opportunity in silk and started the colorful Thai silk industry. It became popular around the world and added much to the Thai economy. It brought him fame and fortune, and his home was a masterpiece of work at that time. In 1965, while on a vacation in northern Malaysia, he disappeared and was never found. There were several clandestine stories of what might have happened to him, but one thing for sure is that he lived a full and exciting life and the people of Thailand considered him a national treasure.

After touring the house, we went to the Jim Thompson silk store and the silk cloth on display was amazing with the many designs and colors. You could purchase silk cloth or ready-made dresses, shirts, purses, and many other things. The prices matched the beauty of the silk, but this was the only place you could buy the real Jim Thompson silk.

I had heard a lot about the pure gold chains and bracelets you could buy in Thailand, so our next stop was in Chinatown where all the gold shops were. There were plenty of shops with gold necklaces hanging off the walls and gold bracelets in the display cases. I purchased a couple of 22-karat gold pieces before we left. The price of a piece was based on the weight of the gold in it and then you negotiated what you were willing to pay for the labor to make it. Pure 24-karat gold is soft and the clasps that hold the bracelet or necklace together bend easily

RANDOM TANGENTS

so you could easily lose the piece. If you were going to buy 24-karat gold it was best to buy it in small bars or as coins.

As it was getting late again, the driver asked if I wanted to go to a club and see a show and I agreed, not knowing what kind of show he was talking about. We arrived at this bar with a stage on one side, sat down, and ordered a couple of beers. The girls started coming over to talk; they seemed to all know him. After a couple of beers, the show began, and it was nothing I had ever seen before. The girls would step up on stage and perform different sexually explicit acts.

One girl was shooting a blowgun with a dart in it and bursting a balloon. Somehow, she compressed the air in her vagina and then shot it out through the blowgun, thus bursting the balloon. Wow! We were having a great time—drinking beer and laughing. Before long, the show started again with the same routine. This time they picked someone from the audience—me! —to come up and hold the balloon while the young lady shot it. I just put the balloon in my teeth and bent over slightly so she could get a good shot at it. The crowd roared as the balloon burst! My Thai driver never laughed so hard and said I was the craziest American he had ever met.

After a few days in Bangkok, I wanted to go to Chiang Mai to see northern Thailand and possibly go to some of the surrounding towns. At that time, the Chiang Mai Orchid Hotel was supposed to be the best place to book a room in, so that's where I ended up. The accommodation was nice, and the staff were very friendly but didn't speak English as fluently as the staff at the Bangkok hotel did. That was fine; we just laughed a lot when we talked and were able to communicate enough to get the idea across.

CUTTING LOOSE: TRUK LAGOON

I rented a car and driver while in Chiang Mai, as I found this to be the easiest way to get around. My driver spoke pretty good English. We visited several of the Buddhist temples and some of the mountain tribes around Chiang Mai. One of them was the Padaung tribe, or Long Neck tribe, as many called them. They had rings around their necks that they kept adding to. In time, this causes the neck to stretch, thus the long necks and the many rings. Another tribe we stopped to see was the Karen tribe. I watched as the women were weaving fabric made of cotton they grew. The dresses and skirts were made differently for a married woman versus a single woman. At least you could tell who was married and who wasn't! I purchased a couple of these maiden dresses to take back to the U.S. as gifts for a couple of single friends.

The next day we took off into the country. I asked if it was true that they had restaurants that served monkey brains. I was thinking about the movie *Raiders of the Lost Ark*, where they were eating monkey brains. I had also heard of street vendors in Taipei or Hong Kong where you could select a live snake and they would kill it and cook it for you. (The latter I knew was true as guys from my unit in Vietnam had seen it while on R&R.) The driver took me to a restaurant away from the city. They had monkeys with collars on them, tied to the trees, a bear in a deep pit, and a large king cobra in another. I asked the driver if the restaurant served these animals. He just nodded and gave me a copy of the menu. It was in Thai so that didn't tell me anything, but I imagine money talks, and if you want to eat monkey brains, no problem.

As we headed back to Chiang Mai, we stopped by a group of artisan shops. Each had its own specialty—silver, jewelry, pottery, and more. At the silver shop I bought a mug for a friend back home and had his name engraved on the bottom. They made these silver bowls and mugs by melting down silver coins. Once the bowl came out of the mold, they filled the inside with hot pitch. Once the pitch cooled, they could engrave the silver without bending it inward. After the engraving was completed, the bowl was reheated, the pitch ran out, and the silver was cleaned.

The next day was Saturday and there was an open-air market going on, so I thought I would walk about and have a look. There was a tub of live eels from the river, large round bugs, bamboo stuffed with sticky rice, and beans cooking on an open fire. They would press the sticky rice and beans out of the hollow bamboo stick onto a plate after it was cooked. I tried that, but gave the bugs and eels a miss. They had about anything and everything imaginable at this market besides food.

After dinner in the hotel, I decided to see what was going on in town. The doorman at the hotel waved for a taxi and told the driver that I wanted to have a few beers and some fun. We stopped at a tall building (at least tall for Chiang Mai) and took an elevator up to the fifth floor. When we got off the elevator, there was a bar and another glass-covered room with girls sitting behind the glass. I noticed an attractive girl who really started smiling at me. I thought, "Why not?" This massage was a little different, as the hot water heater had broken so they had no warm water. She said she would massage me with baby powder instead. Okay! Next, I was lying on a massage table, and she was sprinkling baby powder all over my body. She rubbed it in with her bare breasts. (She had beautiful breasts.)

I asked her why she was working here, and she said that she and her sister wanted to open a beauty salon, and she needed to make money to start their business. She was a beautiful young lady, spoke good English, and had a charming personality. The name on her lapel pin was Po, a name I will not forget.

Since 1983, tourism has taken over this part of Thailand. When I went back in 2018 after thirty-five years, Chiang Mai wasn't what I remembered. It was much more crowded and the traffic heavier thus creating a cloud of pollution that hung over the city. It wasn't free to go into the Paduang Village anymore and you had to pay to get into some of the Buddhist temples, too. Tourism changes everything and Chiang Mai was bustling with tourists and fancy painted tour buses everywhere; it was no longer a laid-back town. There were still some nice things to see there but prices for things had also gone up in relation to the number of tourists.

Hong Kong

The next morning, I caught a flight to Bangkok so that I could catch my flight to Hong Kong in a couple of days. Hong Kong was going to be a new adventure, and I was looking forward to it. Why Hong Kong? Well, my travel agent back in the U.S. told me that I had to go there to experience it as she had been a Pan Am stewardess during the Vietnam war and was stationed out of Hong Kong. She also mentioned that while there, I should look for the beautiful cloisonné pottery and carved ivory.

I arrived and stayed in a hotel just across from the historic Hong Kong Peninsula Hotel. I stopped by the Peninsula Hotel one day for morning tea, which included tea and scones with cream and jam. It was impressive. About two blocks behind the Peninsula Hotel there was a little shop that sold cloisonné pottery and upstairs they had a room full of carved ivory. Some of the ivory carvings were made from complete tusks. At that time, ivory pieces had to be registered as being carved before a certain date in order to be legally sold.

I purchased several pieces of the cloisonné pottery; it was hard to find at that time. The cloisonné vase I bought was an intricate wire sculpture with clay worked into the wire. The piece was fired with different colored glazes. These vases usually came with a small wooden display stand. Also in Hong Kong you could get a three-piece suit tailored and delivered to your hotel in a couple of days. They were 100 percent wool and quite reasonable in price. Hong Kong shopping was a 24/7 deal and you could go out any time of the night and shop.

As I wandered around, I found a German pub. They would take three or four minutes to draw a beer to let the head reside before topping it off. Also, they had several kinds of schnapps in a small freezer. I had started smoking the tasty clove cigarettes from Indonesia. When I lit one up, I was quickly told to smoke a real cigarette, and one of the gentlemen there handed me a packet of Marlboros. That was the end of my clove cigarettes! I started drinking with the guys and the next thing I know we are doing shots of ice-cold apple schnapps!

As the night was young, the next stop was the Kangaroo Pub, which was, you guessed it, an Aussie pub. The fellows I was drinking with also knew the owner. I noticed an attractive lady sitting at the bar having something to eat and finally got the courage up, in liquid form, to go over and talk to her. Her name was Suki and she was a Korean airline stewardess working on Thai Airways who flew the Bangkok-Hong Kong route. She spoke English, Korean, and two dialects of Chinese, and was going to be in Hong Kong for a couple of days. She volunteered to show me around the next day. I couldn't pass that invitation up!

CUTTING LOOSE: TRUK LAGOON

The next day Suki and I took the Star Ferry from Kowloon to Hong Kong Island. Back then everyone rode the Star Ferry across the bay, as it was only $.25 to ride one way on the top deck or $.10 on the lower deck. As we got off the ferry, I noticed an elderly Chinese woman go up to a Mrs. Fields cookie stand and give the girl $.10 for a big cookie, even though the cookies were normally a dollar. This reminded me of Chiang Mai, where people would charge a nickel for a bowl of soup, but if you didn't have the nickel, they would give it to you anyway. That was before tourism and the almighty dollar took over. It was always good to see people who still had kind hearts.

We went for a walk and ended up taking the tram up to Victoria Peak, which offered a panoramic view of the skyline and harbor. From there we went to Ocean Park on the back side of the island, which had some rides and entertainment. It was a great day and I got to see a lot of Hong Kong, but it was time to head back to the U.S. as I had been gone for two months. I had seen a lot of this part of the world that I wished to see and experience, and I was also able to work in some incredible scuba diving.

In 1983 tourism was quickly changing the world as it was becoming easier to reach many of the destinations and tourism was a money maker. The cultures were adapting to tourism and the influx of money. Travel, technology, and capitalism were impacting everything, and change would only accelerate over the years to come.

CHAPTER EIGHT
Adventure Bound: New Zealand

Once back in the States I spent time with my family and my children thinking that I could finish the paperwork pertaining to my divorce and go on with my life. My children and I always enjoyed being together; going out for breakfast on the weekends was a special time we looked forward to. However, it soon turned out that things still were not going anywhere with the divorce as my wife's attorney was dragging it out. I didn't want to just wait around in limbo, so I decided to take a trip to New Zealand and Australia to see some country and do some more diving.

By this time, it was springtime down under. I flew into Auckland and stayed a couple of days before renting a car so that I could drive around the North Island. While in Auckland, I checked out the local pubs and beer. The pub I went to put little baskets of chips on the bar for something to nibble on. It was the first time I had ever had salt and vinegar chips! They made you want to drink more beer, so logical.

New Zealand was beautiful, quaint, and different from the tropical islands I had visited earlier. After renting a car I drove to Rotorua, which is toward the middle of the North Island. As I drove into the valley, I started smelling the sulfur generated from the thermal activity in the valley. The smell reminded me of Yellowstone Park in the U.S.

I looked at a history display of the forests in New Zealand. One of the park rangers said that New Zealand used to be full of massive trees, but when people started arriving, they clear-cut the forests so they could farm and raise sheep. Now they needed a lot of wood pulp to make paper for newspapers, toilet paper, boxes, and other consumer goods. He said they had performed research to find out what species of tree would grow best and quickest in their climate. They ended up planting California pine as it would reach maturity in twenty-eight years. What a project! You never give it too much thought when you go to the toilet (or dunny as it is called in Australia).

I traveled to the South Island of New Zealand to Christchurch and down the coast to a small fishing village called Dunedin. I thought I would indulge in some fresh seafood while on the coast and maybe have a beer or two. I went to a local restaurant close to the wharf and started talking to one of the fishermen there. He told me about the fish they were shipping to the U.S. called orange roughy. He said they used to throw it back into the ocean after catching them because they considered it trash fish. Then someone came up with the brilliant idea to sell it to the Yanks. Instant success! He just couldn't stop laughing.

Australia

After driving back up to Christchurch, I caught my flight to Melbourne, Australia. On touching down, I booked into a hotel and contacted Barb, the lady I had met in Bali. We went out to dinner that night, along with her two children, and had a nice time. She was a positive and fun person and we stayed in contact over the years.

From Melbourne, I traveled to Sydney. It was vibrant! My first stop was the Sydney Opera House to witness the architecture and engineering and later went to the top of the Sydney Tower for a view of the city and the harbor. The next day I visited the Sydney Harbor Bridge and an area called The Rocks, which is part of the old historic district, close to the bridge, and deals with the history of the convicts, soldiers, and sailors who settled in Australia. They also had some nice pubs there for an afternoon lunch and a few beers. Later that day I traveled over to King's Cross, a district in Sydney, to have a look around and stopped in a bakery to see if they had some hot cross buns, a local specialty. They had some out of the oven that were still warm. Of course, I tried a couple with butter and jam; they were delicious. King's Cross had a reputation of being a little more of a shady area of town but it also had some good music and bars along with a few working ladies.

The next day I took a ferry over to Manly Beach and noticed straight away the long line at the ice cream shop. It seems Aussies love their ice cream. I went to the beach before heading back; the water temperature was much cooler here than farther up north on the reef. Altogether, Sydney was a huge melting pot of nationalities. I enjoyed it, but it was time to move on.

I took a flight to Ayer's Rock in the middle of the outback. The name used now for Ayer's Rock is Uluru, its Aboriginal name. A picture of it was on all the tourist brochures and it looked spectacular, so I booked a room at the resort there for three nights. We were driven by bus the next morning to Ayer's

Rock. Some of us were willing to climb it, but the first hundred yards was steep. They had pipes drilled into the rock with a chain linking them together, so you could pull yourself up. The rock monolith stood about 1,150 feet above the desert floor and it took me about thirty minutes of steady climbing to make it to the top. Later, I was told that a lad had made it to the top in twelve minutes, but he happened to be a marathon runner. Today, no one can climb Ayer's Rock as it is considered a sacred Aboriginal site. It is probably a good thing as two or three people would die every year from trying to climb it (usually older people with heart problems). At that time there were no flight for life or emergency teams in the area so medical attention was limited.

After coming back down, we walked around the base of the rock and were shown all the Aboriginal carvings and paintings. We were told that the rock was sitting in a big bowl and when it rained, the water would accumulate in the bowl under the rock. The aboriginals knew this and knew how to extract the water. As we followed each other around the base of the rock, I noticed that there were at least fifty flies on the backs of everyone walking in front of me. Now I understood why Aussies had big hats with corks hanging off the brim and a scarf around their neck. It was quite annoying when the little buggers climbed into your ears or up your nose.

The next day we took a day trip out into the Olga Mountains, which is a small mountain range close to Uluru. It could be a desolate, hot, and dry place in the summer months. Early in the morning it was quite pleasant, though, and in the evenings it would cool off quite a lot as happens in the desert.

From Ayer's Rock, I flew to Cairns to explore the Great Barrier Reef, which was supposed to be one of the best diving spots in the world. The dive shops in Cairns had three-day boat trips, loaded with people going out to do their open water dive certification. I wasn't interested in being in a big crowd, so I opted out. I drove on up north to Port Douglas, about thirty-five miles north of Cairns on the coast, to see what was going on there. An operation called the Quicksilver had a large catamaran that took 140+ people out to pontoons they had anchored at the reef. They served a fantastic lunch while you were out there and you could swim, scuba dive, or go for a little cruise in their glass-bottomed boat to see the fish and the reef. It was a good day trip to get the feel of being out on the reef, but not for serious diving.

While in Port Douglas, I went to the only dive shop there and was able to book a one-day dive trip out to the reef. The boat took a maximum of six divers and was fitted with twin outboard engines, so it made it out to the reef in good time. We loaded some scuba tanks in the boat the next morning and off we went for the day. It took a little less than two hours to get to the first diving spot along one of the reefs. After the dive we anchored inside a small lagoon for lunch. It was a magical day—great weather, warm water, and pretty good diving. We did another dive after lunch and then headed back. The ocean was being kind as the waves weren't bad, and the ride back was smooth.

In 1983 the little town of Port Douglas had two pubs on its main street: the "top pub" and the "bottom pub." Aussies joked about doing a pub crawl between the two pubs especially on Friday or Saturday night. Often one or two guys would end up in the ditch that ran alongside the road between the two pubs. They were usually trying to make their way from one to the other but couldn't quite navigate standing up, so they crawled;

thus it was literally a *pub crawl*. I thoroughly enjoyed Australia and the people as they had a great sense of humor, loved their grog, and stress wasn't in their vocabulary.

Tahiti

By this time, it was time for me to jump on a plane to my next stop: Tahiti. I had first heard of it on the TV show *Adventures in Paradise* with the character Adam Troy and his 85-foot schooner, the *Tiki*. Also, Marlon Brando filmed *Mutiny on the Bounty* there and lived on an island he owned in the vicinity. Even the name Tahiti sounded magical so I thought I would do some exploring.

We landed at Papeete, the capital of Tahiti. When booking into the beachside hotel, the young Tahitian men would take your bags and carry them to your room if you wished. They usually wore no shirts and had the typical Tahitian sarong wrapped around them. The young men at this hotel were in decent shape, had tribal tattoos around their arms, and seemed to be needed quite frequently by the older ladies.

Later, while sitting at the bar of the hotel I noticed that the bartender was dressed like a woman, but she had an Adam's apple. I was told that in the past they used to sacrifice young maidens to the Gods so soon there was a shortage of girls, and they started raising some of the boys as girls.

The next morning, I went down to the wharf and marina in Papeete and checked out the sailing boats. One sailing boat, about fifty feet in length, was just coming into port and was tying up at the wharf. The guy was at the helm guiding it in so that his crew of three ladies could tie it up to the pier. What a tough life this guy had!

RANDOM TANGENTS

Later, I ran into the manager of the hotel where I was staying, and we started talking about things to do in Papeete. She said that I should go out and experience the nightlife. She told me that a friend of hers would be glad to show me around. She said he was gay, but she would tell him I was straight, so everything would be cool. I met this fellow a little later on, and we started off in a bar that had music and dancing. Many of them were gay, so I didn't really feel comfortable, so we left and went to another bar to have a drink.

There I noticed an attractive Tahitian girl with a gorgeous tan. She came up to the bar, so I asked if I could buy her a drink. As we sat down and started to talk, the guy I was with motioned for me that he had something to say to me privately. "What's up?" I asked. "Are you aware that this girl isn't a girl?" he asked me. Geez, Louise! I ran out the back door, shaking my head. This whole night was getting out of control for me. I had never seen so many cross dressers, transvestites, and gays in one place. It was time to head back so I left and went down to a taxi stop. It had been a long evening and I couldn't wait for the taxi to get me back to my hotel.

The next day I was on a ferry over to the next island called Moorea. I thought this would be a better place to hang out for a couple of days and maybe do some diving. I made a reservation for two dives at the hotel where I was staying. The dive master picked me up and then we stopped to pick up another guy. The two of them started talking in French, which I couldn't understand. When something was said about Truk Lagoon, I mentioned I had recently been there. Both started speaking English then! From then on, we had quite a discourse about different dive spots we had been to.

ADVENTURE BOUND: NEW ZEALAND

We did two dives that day, but the reef was dead and gray. There was no prolific fish life to see, only a couple of small reef sharks. I believe the pollution from the island as well as overfishing caused a lot of this. I have heard that there is a little patch of coral at Bora Bora that is worth diving but I most likely will never know.

That night I met the girl who oversaw the entertainment at the resort, and we hit it off right away. She was from California, had green eyes, blond hair, and loved to party. Little did I know then that she would reappear in my life at a later date! I left early the next morning to catch the ferry back to Papeete to get to the airport. I made it there and was sitting waiting for them to call us to board the aircraft, and the next thing I knew some lady was shaking me to wake up. I barely made it on the plane! I was so glad to leave Papeete. Nothing that I experienced here would make me want to come back.

CHAPTER NINE
Into the Fire

I landed in San Francisco on my way back and booked a hotel room close to the airport as I was supposed to fly out the next day to Denver. When I was checking into the hotel, I started talking to the beautiful young lady, named Jill, at the reception. She seemed interested in all my travels, so we had a drink after she got off work, and I ended up flying out two days later. I didn't know then that I would see her again soon.

When I arrived back to Denver, my divorce was still loping along, and I decided to sit my wife down at my parents' house one Sunday evening and iron out an agreement that we could both live with. The next morning, I get a phone call.

"Hello, this is Greg."

"Greg, this is your attorney. I quit."

"What are you talking about?"

"Your wife's attorney has already been to the judge this morning, and they have a $100,000 warrant out for your arrest. Allegedly, you put your wife under duress in coming up with an agreement. What did you do?"

"I had her come over to my parents' house, we went downstairs and came up with a ten-point agreement that I thought was fair."

INTO THE FIRE

"What were you thinking? I am done, you will have to find someone else to represent you."

I hung up the phone and thought for a minute. First, I called Jill to see if she wanted a roommate for a while. Luckily, she seemed enthusiastic. Then I called my travel agent and got a one-way fare to San Francisco leaving out of Colorado Springs. I figured with a $100,000 warrant the police would be watching the Denver airport, so I booked the ticket under an alias name as identification wasn't required back then.

I arrived in San Francisco that evening and took a taxi from the airport over to Jill's place. As soon as I got up to her apartment, she received a phone call from some guy who had been harassing her and breathing deep into the phone. He said he was right across the street watching her. I immediately ran down the stairs and saw a guy taking off from a phone booth across the street. He was far ahead of me, so I couldn't catch him, but he got the message and he never called her again.

We spent some great time together in San Francisco visiting different parts of the town to enjoy all the different types of ethnic food. Of course, we went down to the San Francisco wharf, took the Nob Hill trolley, visited art galleries, and sampled chocolate at Ghirardelli's—all the tourist things. While Jill worked during the day, I walked a lot from Haight Ashbury to Golden Gate Park, around Chinatown, and down to the financial district. San Francisco also had a great bus system, so it was easy to get around.

One day I was looking at her bookshelf and I saw the book *There Is a River* by Tom Sugrue. It was a fascinating book about a devout Christian, Edgar Cayce, who would go into a trance and give medical readings to people who didn't even have to be in the vicinity. He gave over 14,000 readings during his life, and you can still find them online today. One of the areas he delved into was reincarnation. In one of his trance readings he said that he was shown where reincarnation is mentioned in the Bible, even though most Christians don't know how to interpret these passages. When the Bible was put together and edited, most references to reincarnation had been removed. I wasn't surprised at all. How could the Church control people through fear if they knew about reincarnation? This got me thinking, so I started researching different religions and their messages. It was the beginning of a lifelong journey.

I stayed in San Francisco for three months, which went right through Christmas. I was missing my children and family very much by this time and not seeing them at Christmas was the ultimate downer. Jill and I made the best of it and decorated a small tree and had a wonderful dinner together. At least we had each other as she didn't have any family who were close. Finally, in February I contacted my wife to have her drop the warrant so I could come back and hopefully resolve this whole mess. She agreed, and I headed back to Denver. My time in San Francisco will never be forgotten as Jill became close to my heart, but I needed to get things straightened out.

My divorce was coming to a head. By then, I was on my third attorney. This time I supposedly hired the best attorney in Denver. However, at the hearing the big-gun lawyer sent his underling to represent me and she hadn't even opened my file before walking into the courtroom. I had to tell her what questions to ask. I had put up a $5,000 retainer and this was what I got? In the end, the court's decision was for me to send all my money from the sale of my business as well as from the sale of my car to the court, and they would dispense it as they saw fit.

INTO THE FIRE

I started to realize that my interpretation of the American Dream was something I would probably never realize. My dream was to marry someone I loved and who loved me, have a family, pay off the house, get the kids raised, and retire and spend my last days enjoying life with my wife, children, and grandchildren. Even though this dream had mostly evaporated, I had two wonderful children and, luckily, I got to spend quality time with them even during the divorce. I would never change that for anything else.

At this point I just needed to get away and start anew. Work around Denver was basically nonexistent, so I needed to find something to do somewhere else. I knew it wasn't going to be easy leaving my children and family behind, but I didn't want to deal with the anger anymore. I decided to travel back to New Zealand and Australia to see if I could find or start another business there.

Years later I finally realized that the anger you hold inside about some event must be released or it will consume you. After the war and after my divorce, I was holding on to anger that I needed to get rid of. I made the decisions that got me into the predicaments, so I needed to accept them and move on. What was my answer? Forgive yourself! Forgive the ones you were angry with and wish them all the happiness in the world as you move forward. You can do this by living in the present. Life is too short to carry anger, and you can't change yesterday.

CHAPTER TEN
Starting Over: Australia

In 1984, I landed in New Zealand—where this book started. Molly, as you will recall, introduced me to the gypsy woman who laid out her predictions of things to come. I was now having to think seriously about my future and what laid ahead.

My relationship with Molly started to become serious; starting a business in New Zealand seemed like a good plan. When I asked Molly about it, she said that I should speak to her father first.

We drove to Whanganui on the coast, where her parents lived. We had dinner with her family and spent the night. The next day her father and I drove around Whanganui and had a lengthy discussion about New Zealand, the government, and what it would mean for me to start a business. In the end he said the better opportunity was in Australia as there was less government control than in New Zealand. New Zealand was British-orientated, not all that progressive, and taxes were high.

Molly and I traveled on to Wellington and took the ferry to the South Island and drove to Mt. Cook. There was still a little snow on the ice glacier at the top of the mountain and they offered tourists plane rides up to the glacier for a walk. We paid the fare and took off. The plane had ski runners on it so we

STARTING OVER: AUSTRALIA

could land safely on the glacier. During winter you could even attach your skis under the wings and ski down. We got out, took some pictures, and played in the snow before flying back. We traveled to Christchurch and stayed at a nice hotel across from Hagley Park and toured the town. One afternoon when we came back, they had a red carpet unrolled from the entry to the elevator. I saw several guys in business suits, standing around like security guards and asked one of them what was going on.

"We are the security detail for the Duke and Duchess of Kent."

"So that is the reason for the red carpet, right?"

He nodded, then looked at me and laughed. "I know where you are from, the United States."

"How could you tell?"

"We don't have cowboy boots like that in New Zealand and your belt buckle is truly cowboy."

I laughed and asked, "So, where are the Dutch and Duchess of Kent from?"

He laughed again. "Sorry, mate, but it is the Duke and Duchess of Kent, not Dutch and Duchess."

We both laughed, then Molly and I caught the elevator up to our room.

It was time to make a decision about my future, and I knew where I needed to go: Australia. We had talked about it and she knew that I needed to go, and Molly had her own plans. Prior to leaving, I took her out and went shopping for a couple of nice dresses, a purse, and some personal items to help her command attention. I wanted to thank her for the time we had spent together. At the airport, tears were running down her face as she handed me a farewell card. She said she would never forget me. I wouldn't forget her either!

Hello, Australia

I landed in Sydney and stayed a couple of days looking around and planning my trip up the coast. I rented a car to go to Cairns and my only worry was driving on the opposite side of the road. I had done alright in New Zealand, so I figured I could handle it, even with the heavier traffic.

On my way up, I stopped at several places. This was a 1,500-mile trip so I was in no rush and wanted to see the country. You hear so much about the Gold Coast and Sunshine Coast with beautiful beaches, surfing, and nightlife to go along with it. They were both picturesque.

As I continued my drive up the coast on Highway A1, I stopped at Mackay and went out to the harbor. I drove by a grass field with an antique Tiger Moth airplane sitting in the middle. There was a sign that read: "Rides for $40." I had to try this! The owner said he had put a completely rebuilt continental motor in it and for an extra $20, he would do some aerobatic maneuvers over the ocean. I handed him $60, got seated, buckled up, and put my leather helmet on. The pilot hooked up a hose to the side of my leather helmet so that he could talk to me as he flew the plane.

After getting me situated, he grabbed the wooden prop, gave it a spin, and she started right up. He jumped in his seat behind me and away we went. We flew over the ocean and he pulled the plane into a steep climb to the point that the prop stopped. What the hell? He shouted to me that we were in a hammerhead stall. The plane started falling to the left and as

STARTING OVER: AUSTRALIA

we started down, the wind caught the prop and began to spin it, which started the engine again. This was one of the biggest thrills in my life. I had always like roller coasters, but this was beyond that. What a ride!

Next stop on my way up the coast was Townsville, where I stopped to see what kind of dive shops they had. There was a nice shop called Mike Ball's Watersports. I met Mike Ball himself, and we talked for a while. I mentioned I was interested in getting into the diving business and questioned him about Townsville. His answers were vague as he didn't want anyone on his turf and I understood that.

Mike had a catamaran called *Watersport* on which he took up to twenty-eight divers out to the reef on three-day trips. I thought I would give it a try to see what the reef was like out of Townsville. The boat was mostly filled with diving students going out for their open water certification. We left early, and it took us a long time to get to where we were going to dive on the reef. Once out there we did some diving and I noticed how the crown-of-thorns starfish were destroying the reef; they were sucking the life right out of it. This starfish doesn't have a natural predator, so marine biologists and researchers were trying to find a way to stop it. One solution was for divers to go out and pull as many as they could off the reef and bring them back to shore to dry out and die.

We did four day dives and a night dive during the trip. The diving was not as good as I had expected. On our way back, the ocean got rough due to a storm. All the divers were in the saloon after lunch and were watching a movie as the boat was heading back at a slow pace fighting the waves. The boat was bobbing from side to side, and after a while I noticed I was the only one left in the saloon. After the movie was over, I went out onto the back deck to get some fresh air. All I could smell was vomit! Everyone was sick and lying around the back deck in case they had to spew over the side. We finally made it back to the wharf that evening. I could hardly walk straight as I had sea legs from the side-to-side movement of the boat. It took me all evening to get acclimated to walking on land.

Soon, I left Townsville and headed to Cairns to experience yet another part of Australia. Starting at Cairns and going north is a piece of Australia that has a rain forest and a small mountain range covered with lush vegetation. The first Australians who lived in this area cleared the flats, which were part of the rain forest, to raise sugar cane. Today there are still sugar cane fields, but they harvest the cane with modern equipment. Some of the farmers still burn the leaves of the sugar cane prior to harvest and it is a sight to see. They light the cane on fire at one end of the field and it burns fast and hot until it reaches the other end. When it gets there, it completely dies out. While it is burning, hawks circle above, waiting for rats and other varmints to come running out. The ash from the burning sugar cane travels for miles and settles on everything. It is quite the experience, especially if they light it at sundown—you can see the glow for miles.

When I arrived at Cairns, I booked into a hotel a couple of blocks off the waterfront and started exploring. I walked around town and down to the boat docks. It was like walking back in time as the shops shut down at 5:00 p.m. and the grocery stores were only open for half a day on Saturdays. The store windows had mannequins that were from the 1950s! Cairns wasn't unique; most of the towns along the coast and inland had yet to be infected by tourists. The pace of life was

STARTING OVER: AUSTRALIA

still slow and on an even keel. The experience was a breath of fresh air before the impact of tourism.

There were several old pubs around town and the ones close to the main wharf were colorful. The fishermen off the trawlers would often be at the one called the Barbary Coast. Many of the fishermen had tattoos, wore shorts, singlets, and either flip-flops or gum boots. They were a rough-looking crowd, but they were friendly and loved their beer—or grog as they called it.

I started looking around at the boats, thinking about taking people diving on the Great Barrier Reef as a business. I noticed a boat broker's office down at the harbor, so I stopped by. His name was Ian and he said they had a boat for sale lying at anchor in the harbor. It was about seventy-eight feet in length and had been used as a dive boat before but was in rough condition. He said that $25,000 could get it back in top shape.

We took his sixteen-foot runabout and to have a look. The boat had a caulked birch deck and you could tell it had been leaking water. The cabins needed redoing and the engine room was a mess. I didn't know anything about boats, but I was getting ready to learn a hard lesson.

The previous owners from Sydney had bought the boat a year earlier for $165,000. They had someone else running it for them as a dive boat who was taking all the money, performing no maintenance, and running the ship into the ground. They were desperate just to get out of it, so I offered $85,000 for it. They quickly flew up from Sydney and signed the papers. Now I was the proud owner of *Si Bon*, supposedly meaning "she's good" in French. I took it as a good sign.

I hired a young lad part time to help me clean it up. First, we pulled all the chain out of the chain lockers and removed all the handrail. We put a new chain in and had the anchors galvanized. It had an old brass winch, which we took apart, cleaned, and polished; it looked like new. Later we put a new dive compressor on board and piped it for the filling station for our scuba tanks on the back deck. In a rear cabin closet we put in a four-bottle bank system for storing compressed air to help us fill tanks more quickly between dives.

I hired a marine woodworking contractor to refinish all the cabins and the salon with maple veneer before putting down a new carpet. We fiberglassed over the birch deck to eliminate any more leaks into the cabins. Everything was coming together. A new handrail and duck board or scuba diving platform at the stern of the ship were the finishing touches along with a new paint job from the deck up.

One day while we were tied up alongside the wharf while the ship was stripped down with no anchors and only one engine that ran, the pier master said I had to get off the wharf to allow a larger vessel in. Even though I had never driven the boat before, I had to start up the engine. The lad helping me untied us, and I gently took the ship out into the middle of the inlet waiting to see where this other ship was going to tie up.

While waiting out in the middle, the engine died and there wasn't enough battery power left to turn it over, so we were dead in the water. By this time, I was sweating bullets. If the wind blew me one way, I would end up drifting through sailing boats tied to moorings, causing damage. If the wind blew me back toward the wharf, I would crash into one of the vessels tied up there.

Suddenly, a gentle breeze came up and pushed me toward the wharf, so I started dropping all our bumpers off the starboard side. There was a row of ships and a space of about ninety feet that was still open between them. The breeze pushed us

STARTING OVER: AUSTRALIA

exactly into that space! We tied up as though it was all planned and I still think about it today that a finger must have come from out of the sky and pushed us exactly into that space. There was no insurance on *Si Bon*—it could have been a total disaster. Six months later, with about $80,000 invested into the refit, it was about to be finished. I was close to being out of money by this time, so I ended up flying to Sydney and cashing in my gold jewelry I had bought in Thailand to finish paying for the refit. At this time I formally named my new business, Fantasy Dive Charters, since we were going to be doing dive charters on the Great Barrier Reef. I also took on a partner named Mike, who owned the dive shop in Port Douglas. He was there to help me secure a loan so I could have some operating capital to get the business started. Later, I would buy him out. The boat was free and clear, but the bank wanted an Australian citizen's signature on the loan. Mike had just taken his tests to qualify for running a ship this size, so things seemed to be working out.

I decided to take a couple of weeks off to go back to the U.S. and see my kids and family. I had pulled *Si Bon* into a shipyard and hauled her out of the water so I could power wash the bottom and paint it while balancing the two thirty-inch propellers. I would put her back in the water once I returned. (My Australian multiple entry visa required me to leave the country every six months, so I made a trip back to the U.S. to see my children and family every six months.)

When I arrived in the states a friend told me that that my old competitor in the concrete business, Mary, was going through a divorce. She had settled with her ex and was stressing out drinking Coke, chain smoking, and not eating properly. I met with her and told her to grab a plane ticket and come to

RANDOM TANGENTS

Australia for a while to unwind. She thought that was a great idea and booked a ticket for a few weeks later.

When I returned, I relaunched the ship. A few days after taking *Si Bon* back to Port Douglas, a young Swedish lady came into the dive shop. Her name was Anna and she wanted to book a dive trip to the reef for five days. She was told we needed eight people to book a trip to Lizard Island and back at $600 per person. The next day she came back with seven people! She had found three other young ladies and four guys—none of whom had met each other before. It blew me away that she could find seven people ready to go on a trip so quickly. She was passionate and didn't take no for an answer.

The trip was for five days and we did a lot of diving and spent some time on Lizard Island before returning. After the first three days everyone started warming up to each other, and by the time we hit Lizard Island, Mike had made it known to the ladies that he was available, which struck a wrong chord with me as I knew that he was married with children at home. I could tell this business relationship was going to be short-lived. However, the trip was a good first run for *Si Bon* to see how everything was working and reveal what required fixing.

When we returned, we let everyone off at the public wharf in Port Douglas and I anchored *Si Bon* up the river, which was mainly covered with mangrove swamp. I was told that if you heard a sound like a cow bawling at night, it was most likely a croc. They were up in the mangroves, so I wasn't going out for a swim.

I soon ran into Anna again in town and we started talking. I asked if she wanted to stay on *Si Bon* while it was at anchor. She said that would be great, so later that day I took her out. We started having an in-depth conversation about New Age

STARTING OVER: AUSTRALIA

stuff and one thing led to another. She stayed with me on *Si Bon* for a couple of days, and then we decided to head to Cairns and find a hotel to stay in until she headed back to Sweden a week later. We had a lot of fun and enjoyed spending time together. Needless to say, we were getting a little bit involved with each other by this point.

She told me she had recently been making about $10,000 a week as a fashion model and she also worked part time at her father's hotel in Sweden. I wasn't surprised; she was 5'11"—statuesque—with blond hair and blue eyes. She would travel for six months and go back to Sweden for six months to manage the hotel; she modelled in between. She had dived at a lot of places that I wanted to go to; we developed a genuine connection. When she left, she said she would be back in six months to be with me again, and I was looking forward to that. But was the relationship based on lust or love? Sometimes there is a fine line between the two. When she arrived back in Sweden we talked on the phone several times over the next couple of weeks. She told me how much she cared for me and wanted to be with me when she came back. It all sounded good, but things happened fast.

Two weeks after she left, I received a phone call from the green-eyed girl from LA I had met in Tahiti. The gypsy woman was right—she was just about to reappear in my life. Strike one! I don't have a clue as to how she located me, but she was flying into Cairns and asked me if I would meet her. When she came off the plane, she had a cast on her leg and her arm was in a sling. It turned out that she and her boyfriend in New Zealand had been in a car crash. She showed me a picture of the car, which happened to be a station wagon. Strike two! The gypsy woman had told me to beware of a station wagon.

RANDOM TANGENTS

I was trying to figure out how much I really cared for Anna and concluded that I had some deep feelings for her. She was so positive and such a force to be reckoned with—in more ways than one. I let the green-eyed girl stay with me for two days and realized she needed to leave if I was going to try and make it work with Anna. I thought about it constantly and knew this green-eyed girl had no feelings for me beyond having a good time. I asked a friend to take her back to Cairns from Port Douglas and he dropped her off on the beach. My friend said it didn't take her fifteen minutes to hook up with someone new. In the end, those two days she spent with me cost me dearly.

At about the same time, back in Sweden, Anna had gone to a psychic for a reading about me. In her next phone call to me she told me that the psychic had seen me having an affair with a green-eyed girl. She didn't want to talk about it or listen to my side of the story but said she would be back in six months. The phone calls stopped and left me wondering if I could ever mend this relationship. Anna did come back at the end of six months, but the connection wasn't there anymore. She wouldn't listen to my side of the story and how much I wanted to try and make it work. Who knows, maybe that's the way it was supposed to be. Maybe I had a different path to take. You can't live in the past, but I think I should have put more stock into what the gypsy told me: "Beware of a station wagon."

The only catch I had in trying to figure out the feelings I had for Anna was that she was having a fling with a married man I knew when she came to stay on *Si Bon*. Was the quick relationship that we built on a solid foundation or was it just a feel-good time when everything clicked? Sometimes things go up quickly and come down just as quickly, but it still left a void in my heart.

STARTING OVER: AUSTRALIA

A Tough Start

Mary flew into Cairns from Denver shortly after this and I introduced her to several of my friends in Port Douglas. After a week of being there and partying with several of the people, she was loving it. She said she wanted to be a partner in Fantasy Dive Charters, and I told her she had better think about it as she was 10,000 miles from home and her family. She said we could take turns and work six months each and then go back to the States. This seemed like a good compromise, so we bought a white building overlooking the ocean with its own wharf and a fifty-five-foot fishing boat. The gypsy woman was right again! She had mentioned a white house overlooking the ocean. Strike three!

Early one morning, during one of *Si Bon*'s first trips out to the reef, I received a phone call.

"Hello."

"Hello, this is Radio Darwin."

"Yes?"

"Is this Fantasy Dive Charters and do you have a ship named *Si Bon*?"

"Yes, is there a problem?"

"Your captain on *Si Bon* contacted us by radio saying that he was up on a reef and needs assistance. It seems he is hard aground and wishes for you to bring out your fishing vessel to take off the passengers and to arrange a vessel to pull him off."

"Is everyone okay and did he mention the extent of damage?"

"He said everyone was okay and didn't think the ship had a lot of structural damage as it wasn't taking on much water."

"Did he say exactly where they were at?"

"Yes, he said they were on top of the reef just north of your anchorage spot."

"Thank you and can you contact our captain and let him know we are on our way out to him and should be there within four hours?"

"Yes, we will relay the message to him."

"Thank you for your help."

"No worry and we will be back in touch with you if anything else is needed."

"Thank you again."

A few hours later we arrived with our fishing vessel and took everyone off *Si Bon*. The boat had run aground right on top of the reef at high tide and was lying on her side as the tide went out. The passengers all seemed relaxed even after this ordeal. Later I found out that they had a wreck party going on all night during which they drank all the beer and ate all the food, but that was fine.

I stayed on *Si Bon* as the fishing vessel took all the passengers back. She had been operational for less than a month after six long months of refitting and now this! A salvage vessel came out later that evening and tied onto *Si Bon* to the winch on the stern of the salvage ship. The salvage ship captain dropped two anchors off the bow of his vessel, so he wouldn't slip and started winching us off the reef when the tide got to its highest point. The propellers and shafts on *Si Bon* were destroyed and there were a few punctures in the copper-sheathed skin over the timber hull. I had brought out a gasoline-powered pump to use in case the pumps on *Si Bon* weren't operational to pump out any water coming in. It took all night to tow her back to Cairns and get her tied up at the shipyard. They put her up on the slip that day to see the extent of the damage and it was estimated that she was going to be out of the water for six weeks for repairs. It was a good thing we had insurance by then!

I had been designing a brochure for *Si Bon* and Fantasy Dive Charters and it was ready to go to press when she went on the reef. After this, I wasn't going to do any more short and fast student trips. I had spent too much time and money to see her being torn up by the quick turnaround of students, so I wanted longer charters up the Great Barrier Reef and out into the Coral Sea with experienced divers.

After they started working on *Si Bon*, I flew back to the U.S. with a box of freshly printed brochures and started going to dive shops to get them interested in spreading the word. The couple that I had met in Palau, Ray and Beth, had hooked me up with their dive shop in Richardson, Texas so we met up and spent a fun evening together. I ended up with full-boat charters from Richardson, Texas; Salt Lake City, Utah; and Boulder, Colorado. When I returned to Australia, the ship was about finished so we started scheduling six-day trips to Lizard Island every week.

These trips had the same itinerary: we would motor out to Escape Reef for the first night and then work our way up the Ribbon Reefs until we got to the top of number ten Ribbon Reef and dive the Cod Hole on the third day. From there we went into Lizard Island for the night and had a barbecue on the beach. This would allow everyone time to go ashore for a few hours and hike around the island. The next morning, we would head back down the Ribbon Reefs for the remainder of the trip and back into Port Douglas on Saturday morning. There was plenty of diving to do on the 125 miles of reef we traversed. The cost for the six-day trip was $900 Australian dollars, which included accommodation on the ship, meals, and all your dive gear. We even had a van to pick up people in Cairns and return them afterwards.

At the same time, we were trying to keep the fishing vessel going and service the prior owners' clients. It was a good seagoing vessel that the prior owner had built himself; it had twin diesel motors driving it along with a large freezer capacity for the fishing charters. It slept eight passengers and could go out for ten days up the coast and into the reefs for fishing. It wasn't my cup of tea as it was a constant battle trying to keep the boat clean while they were fishing with the bait, fish scales, and innards getting stuck on everything.

Our full-boat charters for *Si Bon* during the height of the season were a ten-day trip up the Great Barrier Reef to Lizard Island and then out into the Coral Sea. We would usually head out from the top of number ten Ribbon Reef at midnight and steam out seventy miles to Osprey Reef, which is about one hundred miles offshore in the Coral Sea. Osprey Reef is like a mountain top sticking out with 6,500 feet of water surrounding it. The wall diving here was great along with all the sharks on Shark Point. Often we would also head north up to Bougainville Reef for a day or two before coming back into the Great Barrier Reef. We would only go out into the Coral Sea during the summer season when the winds changed, and the seas were calmer. This usually started about the end of November and lasted until the end of February. As the water warmed up, you had to monitor the weather closely as a typhoon could form quickly. If the barometer started dropping, it was a good indication that something could be happening, so you stayed on the radio listening to weather reports and making sure everything was okay. This was before we had GPS and weather radar being broadcast from satellites.

STARTING OVER: AUSTRALIA

The ten-day trips took a lot of planning as passengers ate and drank a lot. We had a large freezer for all our frozen food, an ice machine, and two large cooler boxes we packed with vegetables, fruit, and ice. We stored dry goods and jugs of juice under the seats in the salon, so we had every empty space packed. We also caught fresh fish while at sea to supplement your food stores as there was little left at the end of ten days feeding nineteen people. That was fifteen passengers and four crew, which was our maximum complement.

We always stopped at the Cod Hole at the top of number ten Ribbon Reef on all our trips. There was a school of potato cod, about thirty or so, in an area at the top end of the reef. They were about four feet long and docile. I would give divers some small frozen mackerel or sardines that I kept in the freezer so they could handfeed the cod. One day I had my divemaster drop me on the outside of the reef so that I could enter the Cod Hole with the tide. I had never dived this far around on the outside of the reef before and wanted to explore to see what fish life may be out there. Just as I was entering the Cod Hole from the outside, two of the large potato cod swam right by me, which seemed odd. I looked back and there was a shark that they turned away. The same thing happened again out at Bougainville Reef, which is out further in the Coral Sea. They say that you usually never see the shark that attacks you as they tend to come from behind. Were the cod protecting their turf or turning the shark away from me? If only I could read their minds or tune in to their telepathy!

There was also a big fat green moray eel at the Cod Hole that we would hand feed. It had acquired the name Fred and once fed, it would come further out of its hole and you could pet it. Eels are almost blind, so you need to keep your fingers away from their mouth when feeding them. Two small reef sharks also lived there, and you could often find them lying on a sandy area in about forty feet of water next to the reef. After diving there over the course of seven years, one gets familiar with the area and everything that lives there. In time I worked with the Marine Parks out of Cairns, showing them different areas and dive sites they needed to protect on the reef. They in turn set some of the reefs up as no fishing zones and set up anchor points in the Cod Hole to prevent damage from anchors being dropped.

Australian Lady

Everything was going along fine, and Mary was taking her turn going back to the U.S. for her six-month rotation. Soon, I was invited to a wedding. When first working on *Si Bon* in Cairns, I made friends with a pilot who flew a coast watch airplane up and down the coast out of Cairns. He was getting married, so I went dressed in my best pants and a pair of nice Tony Lama cowboy boots. At the church I noticed identical twin sisters sitting in front of me. When everyone arrived at the reception, the emcee asked everyone to take their seats at the table with their name on it. I looked for my name printed on a small card and it just happened to be across from one of the twins. Little did I know at the time that she had set this up with the emcee. Her sister was also there with her husband and another couple. I met everyone at the table and the party was on.

As the night wore on, I danced with this lady and she informed me that she was sort of still involved with a guy back in New York as she had lived there not long ago. I said that was fine and I went back up to the bar to talk to the other guests.

Next thing I knew I got a tug on my sleeve. She wanted to dance again. After the dance she said she would like me to come back and sit with the group, so I did.

As the night wore on, everyone was getting tipsy. She suddenly took a rose out of the vase on the table and placed it in her cleavage. I looked at her and then got up, walked over, bent down, and pulled the rose out with my teeth. That shocked her a bit, but everyone was laughing about it.

Well, that's how it all started between me and my Australian wife, Suzanne. She started coming up to Port Douglas and helping out at the office. In time, I started thinking about what a good friend and mate she was, so we ended up getting married in a little private ceremony in Cairns. She had a young son from a previous marriage, so the gypsy woman was right again. Strike four!

When Mary got back from her six-month stay in the States, she said she was getting homesick and didn't know if she could stand to be away for another six months without seeing her kids and family. We ended up selling the fifty-five-foot fishing boat and the house and wharf on the inlet so that she could cash out. That left me with *Si Bon* and Fantasy Dive Charters, which meant I was back to square one which wasn't all bad. At least now I didn't have to run a fishing charter vessel, which was always a challenge to clean up and keep in shape.

Tragedy at Sea

The following season, after we sold the property on the waterfront, we were booked for several ten-day trips—starting in November and going through February. One of the first trips in November was with a group from Texas; we went up the

RANDOM TANGENTS

Ribbon Reefs then out to Osprey Reef. We arrived at Osprey Reef early in the morning and got everyone up and in the water for an early morning dive before breakfast and then relaxed for a few hours as we enjoyed the calm water and sun. It was a magical day!

The group had their instructor with them, and they were all certified divers. An older gentleman and his wife were friends of the instructor. The wife had come along just for the trip as she didn't dive. Her husband, Bill, had been a hard hat commercial diver and had been diving most of his life. On the second day, Bill partnered up with the instructor to take pictures of reef fish along the wall of the reef. The water was flat and calm, and the reflection of the sky made it look like a mirror.

Thirty minutes after they submerged, Bill came floating to the surface. My two divemasters jumped into our dive tender and hurried over to see what was wrong with him. They pulled him onto our dive tender and took off his dive gear. They started giving him mouth to mouth and CPR. His wife looked on and said, "Is that Bill? Well, that is the way he wanted to go." Then she proceeded down the steps to her cabin and came back with a couple of pills saying he might need these to get his heart going. I couldn't believe my ears. By this time, I had set up the oxygen on the back deck, then jumped into the water and swam over to the dive tender. I took over the mouth to mouth as we motored back to *Si Bon*. I kept working on him for twenty minutes, but I couldn't get him back. His eyes were glassed over, and I knew that was it.

When the instructor got back on *Si Bon*, we asked him what had happened. He said that Bill went straight down, and he caught him at a depth of about one hundred feet, where Bill gave the instructor the okay signal and they headed back up to the forty-foot level. The instructor resumed taking photos, and he only realized something was wrong when he looked up to the surface and saw him floating.

I noticed that all the air was gone from his tank. He had vomited in his mask and inhaled it into his lungs and when that happens, you are a goner. Did he run his air out on purpose, and if he did, why? Things were not adding up! My divemaster told me that at the beginning of the trip he said that he had had an operation six months prior, but he could dive and would take it easy. They had told him to stay within forty feet of the surface.

As we had to wait until the next morning for a plane to transport the deceased back to Cairns, I left the wetsuit on him and put large garbage bags on the body. Then I secured two boat oars down his sides to keep him straight. We laid him on one side of the back deck until the plane landed the next morning. We placed him into a body bag and then loaded him into the plane along with his wife. I also had a divemaster accompany them so that he could file an incident report based on the written report from the whole crew.

The funny thing to me was that the group just sort of glazed over the incident and wanted to go back to diving and kind of forget the whole thing. Maybe it was because they didn't know him before, but I found the attitude a little odd. One never knows for certain how people are going to respond to something like this. I guess life goes on and you keep going, not allowing all the drama to affect you. Does death only affect those closest to you? In fifty or one hundred years you will probably only be a name on a family tree anyway. No emotions, just a name!

RANDOM TANGENTS

We finally got back to shore five days later. After dropping off everyone in Cairns, I went to the airport and asked the police sergeant in charge if I could possibly see the autopsy report. He said he couldn't show that to me, but he said the fellow had less than six months to live as he was full of cancer. The wife had already had him cremated in Cairns and gave the ashes to us to bury him at sea. She also requested that we send her six copies of his death certificate. It seemed that this whole thing had been planned out and our business got stuck in the middle. I kept remembering what Bill's wife said when he came floating to the surface, "Is that Bill? Well, that is the way he wanted to go!" For him, it was probably a good way to die, as there was little suffering, but I wished he had done it somewhere else.

I set his ashes on the mantle above the fireplace in the house we were renting until the next time I was going back out. The next trip was another ten-day trip out to Osprey Reef, so I took the container of ashes onboard *Si Bon* with my personal gear without saying anything to anyone. We followed our usual path up the Ribbon Reefs and anchored up at the Cod Hole until midnight when we picked up our anchor and steamed out to Osprey Reef arriving at daylight. We dived three times that day and anchored up for the evening as we were staying two days. We just happened to be anchored up close to the spot where he had died a few weeks prior. The next morning, at approximately 5:30 a.m., the sun was just coming up and the ocean was calm as I took the container with Bill's ashes to the stern of *Si Bon*. No one was up yet so I carefully opened the container so that I wouldn't spill anything on the deck. I looked up at the rising sun and said a quick prayer as I prepared to spread the ashes out onto the ocean. At the exact time I threw the ashes outward toward the water, a gust of wind came up and blew them right back onto me. It seemed I just couldn't get rid of him! I quickly jumped into the ocean to wash him off not knowing whether to laugh or be pissed off. He probably had the last laugh! After I got back ashore, I sent a letter to his widow telling her that his ashes were buried at sea at sunrise on December the seventh. She wrote back thanking me; he was a veteran and December 7th was Pearl Harbor Day.

More Memories

I have many magical memories from these years! On one of our trips we had a gentleman who had been an Easter Seals poster child. (He had polio when he was a child and he was chosen to be part of their campaign to raise money to fight polio.) We didn't know this until Suzanne picked him and his wife up in Cairns and he had a set of braces he walked with. Although his lower extremities were paralyzed, this gentleman did not let that slow him down. Once everyone was onboard, we were off to go diving. At our first dive spot, he geared up with his wife; he had special round fins that went on his hands. When he got in the water, he was like a fish getting around. It was amazing how someone who grew up with a disability like this made the most of it and had such a positive outlook on life. To him it wasn't so much a disability as he had learned how to deal with it as part of his everyday existence. He didn't let it affect his attitude and he strived to accomplish things others would not dream of. His spirit was intact!

The oldest person we took out was in a group from Salt Lake City for a six-day trip. There was a mother and daughter who came together; the mother was ninety years old. Seeing the Great Barrier Reef was on her bucket list, so off we went. It was a magical week with light seas and beautiful weather. When she first got onboard, she was a little wobbly but had a great attitude. When we stopped to go diving, the crew would get her on the duckboard at the back of *Si Bon* and have her put on a snorkel, mask, and fins. Then they would float out a buoy on a rope, so she had something to hang on to while watching the reef below and around her. There was one stop we could make at the outer edge of a small reef that sat in between two larger reefs in an opening to the ocean. It was like diving into a massive aquarium with thousands of tiny colorful fish and beautiful coral. The crew helped the lady get fitted with snorkeling gear and hung a rope to a buoy right above this beautiful part of the reef. She stayed out in the water for forty minutes just looking around. When she got back aboard, she couldn't stop smiling. She said it was a trip of a lifetime and kept thanking my crew. About a year later we heard that she had passed away, but she took a beautiful memory with her and left one with us as well. She genuinely lived her life to the fullest and didn't let a little age get in her way. It is amazing when people at any age focus on what they *wish* to accomplish and what they *do* accomplish with sheer determination.

Shortly after that trip we had a full-boat charter with a group from France. Since they were going to be out on *Si Bon* for New Year's Eve, I put a case of champagne on board so they could celebrate. We did our standard route; we went to the Cod Hole and then steamed all night to Osprey Reef as the charter wanted to do some wall diving. When everyone woke up and went outside to gear up for the first dive of the day, several of the passengers started to panic. They saw the expansiveness of the great blue ocean with no land in site and realized their own mortality. Being away from a reality that defines you gives you a new perspective. They decided they would do a couple of dives and then head back. We returned to Lizard Island for New Year's Eve. One gentleman in the group was a chef who had his own restaurant in France so when it was time to open the champagne bottles, he took a dull knife and sabered the tops off every one of them. I had never seen that before! Read up on the technique before trying it yourself, though, as there is an art to it. They had a raging party and what a better place to have it than on Lizard Island next to the Great Barrier Reef?

Foretold Warnings

It was 1990 and everything was going well as we had moved inland into a nice house located in the rain forest after having an auction to sell the building and wharf on the waterfront (they auction property in Australia rather than just listing it). One weekend, shortly after moving, my wife and I were invited to go to dinner with her sister and her husband along with a few friends at a hotel where they were all staying. We decided to get a room also as we didn't want to drink and drive. At about 2:00 a.m., after having dinner and a few drinks, my wife and I decided to go and relax in the hot tub. After a while I was getting warm and decided to go and dive into the pool to cool off. It was much shallower than I thought, and I hit the bottom with my head. Suddenly I couldn't move my arms and knew I was possibly paralyzed as I laid on the bottom of the pool. I quickly had an in-depth mental conversation with the man upstairs about how I couldn't die yet as I still had two children who needed me.

RANDOM TANGENTS

I don't know how long I laid on the bottom of the pool but the next thing I knew was that my wife was grabbing me on both sides of my head and lifting me up to give me a kiss. She thought I was just playing around! At that moment I was able to get my feet under me and push myself up onto the edge of the pool. Blood started running down my face from the top of my head due to the big gash on my scalp. Right then I remembered what the gypsy woman had said about a neck injury in or around water! Strike five! I had been so careful out on *Si Bon* not to get a neck injury and when I didn't expect it, whammy.

Suzanne quickly called her sister, a nurse, over to have a look at me. She thought I should go to the hospital right away and get checked out. My alcohol judgement told me that I would be fine, and I would look at my head the next morning. I had started getting movement back in my arms and hands so I thought I would be okay as it was just a temporary thing. It felt as if 10,000 little pins were sticking in my arms, but at least I was still alive.

The next morning, I looked in the mirror and my hair was matted in dried blood so I got in the shower and washed off the best I could. I looked again in the mirror and the top of my head had a large gash, so I knew I needed stitches. When leaving the hotel, I left $100 on the bed to cover the cost of sheets and pillowcases as they were covered with blood from the gash in my head. At the clinic, a traveling doctor from England stitched me up. Every time she tied the knot in the suture, she would yank hard and I was wondering if she knew how sensitive the human head can be. I concluded that she must have been a veterinarian who worked on horses. Later that day, I went to Cairns General Hospital and had some X-rays taken as a precaution. It turned out I had three broken bones and two smashed discs in my neck. They gave me a collar to wear to limit the movement in my neck as it healed and then turned me loose. I was lucky not to be paralyzed and realized how one quick second can change your whole life.

My wife had been working for a chiropractor, so she convinced me to go and see him. It was the right choice as he told me not to lie on the injury as they had me do in the hospital. He started working on my neck gently over the next few months so that I could stay mobile and nothing would fuse.

After a few weeks I ditched the collar and was able to go back out on another six-day diving trip. I had a new skipper on board, and I was teaching him about *Si Bon* and his responsibilities. When we got to the Cod Hole, I took two divers out in our fourteen-foot rubber inflatable runabout over to the outside edge of the reef where they were going to dive. After the divers went down, the motor died on the inflatable. There were ten-foot waves coming into the opening of the reef from the ocean and a current going out. I knew if I stayed in the runabout, I would end up on the next reef upside down on the coral, so I jumped into the water. I was only about one hundred feet from the boat, and I thought I could swim it—no problem.

For some reason, I hadn't put my fins and mask into the runabout, which is standard procedure in case something happens. I wasn't counting on the swift current and the big waves, and without my fins and mask I started floundering in the water. I finally decided to swallow my ego and yell for help. Two guys on the boat grabbed a life ring and came out to get me. My runabout ended up on the next reef over, so we had to go and recover it. It had flipped upside down and the motor was underwater. I nearly died in the water again. This was too close. Why did I keep getting close calls? How many times in my life had death smiled at me and I walked away?

A few weeks later when we were back up at Cod Hole. We lost our hundred-pound plow anchor while pulling it up. The shackle holding it onto the chain came loose and there went the anchor into about one hundred feet of water. I had another anchor so we could continue with the trip as planned. I knew the location where it had dropped and thought that when we came back the next time, I would go down and recover it.

When we arrived back into Port Douglas, I took all our diving regulators to Cairns to a friend of mine who was a diving instructor and asked him to service them for me. He said I could pick them up within a week. On our next trip up to the Cod Hole two weeks later, I took some friends along, including my brother-in-law. When we got to the Cod Hole, I asked him if he would help me recover the anchor that we had lost. We went down and were at a depth of eighty feet when I took a breath of air and suddenly it was all water. My immediate reaction was to try and take another breath, but it was still water. I tried not to panic and reached for my spare regulator, but when I went to put it in my mouth, the mouthpiece was gone. This had never happened to me before. All I had to get air through was a tiny hole about the size of a pencil, so I made a lip seal on that so that I could get some air. The key was not to panic as I had been in a couple of tough spots before, but it is easier said than done, especially when you are eighty feet down.

I tried to attract my brother-in-law's attention, but he just kept on swimming, so I decided to head to the surface while taking my time. I was able to suck enough air through that small opening to make it back to the surface. When I finally got

STARTING OVER: AUSTRALIA

back onboard *Si Bon*, my brother-in-law came to the surface too after realizing I wasn't down there anymore.

I started checking to see why the regulator packed in on me. I opened it up and found a glob of silicon inside that was stuck between the rubber diaphragm and the housing, which let the water in when I inhaled. I was going to have a few words with my friend who supposedly knew how to service them when I got back! I went through all the regulators on the ship and cleaned them all and removed any silicon before I let anyone else dive. Later in the day we went back down, and I was able to recover the anchor.

When we arrived back in Port Douglas, I decided it was time to get out of the water and out of the business. With three close calls in the water in four months, I didn't want to press my luck further. We had been in business for seven years working hard to build it, but it was time to move on. We had experienced so much during this time and made many friends. I put the business up for sale in the Sydney paper during the summer of 1991 and sold it three months later to an English fellow and his two sons.

I stayed around for another three months teaching the young English lads all about *Si Bon*, the routes we took, and the dive spots we went to on our trips. I gave them all the names of skippers we used along with cooks and dive instructors so they wouldn't struggle getting started as I did.

I found out later they didn't take it seriously and thought it was just a party boat, had their girlfriends cook and did not pay much attention to the guests. Their father had all these plans to tap into the Japanese market and have plenty of business. Within a year they weren't paying their fuel bill and finally had to sell out. It was sad to hear that all the work we had put into building the business went down the tube. Looking at this and other businesses that I had been involved in, the businesses took on my spirit or vision as to how the business was viewed and how it operated. After leaving a business and handing it off to someone else than their spirit or vision must be incorporated into the business. It is this transition that will determine whether the original business will prosper or decline. In the past I have seen my own business start to fail by taking my focus off the business at hand. If the strong passion that you once had in making the business a success dissipates due to lack of focus then in time it will have an adverse effect on the business.

Behind the Scenes

I always had people come up to me saying how we had the perfect lifestyle. Little did they know the amount of work that went into keeping things running and how tiring it was to take responsibility for people's lives once they stepped on your vessel. Sometimes it wasn't only the passengers that you had to worry about but also the crew. One time we had hired a new skipper for a trip as all the other ones we normally used were busy that week. After three days we finished diving the Cod Hole and pulled into Lizard Island for the evening to have a barbeque on the beach. After we anchored up one of the passengers, who was a nurse, called me aside to talk to me.

"Do you know that your skipper has a blood pressure problem?"

"No, so what is going on?"

STARTING OVER: AUSTRALIA

"Well he asked me to take his blood pressure and check his heart rate as it seems he left his medication on shore when you left."

"How bad of a situation are we looking at?"

"After checking his blood pressure and pulse he needs to get ashore and see a doctor as soon as possible. He could be looking at a possible heart attack without his medication."

"Thank you for telling me as he hadn't talked to me about any of this. I will take care of the problem as quickly as possible. Can you continue to monitor him until I get a seaplane out here?"

"Yes, that's not a problem and he should just rest and take it easy until you can get him ashore."

I radioed our base in Port Douglas and asked my wife to get in touch with one of our regular skippers, John, and tell him we needed him and that it was an emergency. He was on a seaplane the next morning coming to Lizard Island so I could relieve the other skipper of his duties. I didn't have a choice—the lives of the passengers were at stake along with the life of this skipper.

Several months later, Suzanne and I ran into that skipper while we were having lunch in Cairns. I didn't want to see the guy because he was irate when I relieved him of his command and had him flown back to Cairns. He came to our table and started to talk.

"First, I want to thank you for what you did while I was on your vessel. I know that I was irate after being relieved of my command, but you made the right decision. The fact is if I hadn't gotten back to the doctor when I did there is a distinct possibility I wouldn't be standing here today."

"Did you get back on your medication and get everything under control?"

"It was a little more than that. I had to have open heart surgery very soon after getting back as I was on the verge of a major heart attack due to large blockages in the arteries going to my heart."

"I am glad to see everything turned out for the better and that you are standing here talking to me."

"I just want to say thank you again and there are no hard feelings on my part by the decision that you made. Cheers!"

I really took to heart what he said. One never knows how the decisions you must make are going to affect someone.

Navigation

When I first started taking *Si Bon* up the Great Barrier Reef, we depended on old admiralty charts that showed the reefs and depth of water in fathoms. A fathom is about six feet and was originally measured by dropping a lead weight on a line to the bottom off the side of a vessel. As you pulled the weighted line back up, you would stretch it across your chest from one extended arm to your other extended arm and that length would be one fathom. These charts provided a footnote that said the reefs could be as far as half a mile off from where they were drawn. This was just about the time that satellite navigation was coming into play. Once that and GPS appeared, the world of navigation changed into a more precise science.

The first time we went out to Osprey Reef we were using the old admiralty chart and navigated accordingly. Osprey Reef was an easy target to find as it was about twelve miles long. As we were anchored on the north end one evening, my skipper,

STARTING OVER: AUSTRALIA

John, the same skipper who pulled *Si Bon* off the reef when we first started, used his sextant and shot our position. He told me that the north end of this reef was half a mile off from where it was drawn. Obviously, I had no way of proving him right or wrong without satellite navigation on board. A year later, after we had satellite navigation installed, we went back to the same location and proved he was right within a few meters.

I asked him how the old sailors could draw the reefs if they didn't have an airplane to look down on them. He said that they would anchor their big ship and then take a smaller boat and row around the reef. As they rowed, they would take a position by using their sextant. As they knew how far the crow's nest was above the water, they could use simple geometry and determine their distance from the ship and thus could outline the reef as they went along. Their precision of their calculations and drawings was impressive.

John was one of two skippers who went out with us who were so knowledgeable about the ocean and navigation that you trusted them totally. This was a plus when we first started going out beyond the Great Barrier Reef and into the Coral Sea. They would compute distance and direction by using only a compass and the old admiralty charts we had—then plug in our estimated speed to determine the approximate time of arrival. Getting close to arrival time early in the morning was always tense as you wanted to spot the reef as soon as possible so that you didn't miss it or go aground. If the seas were flat, that would also present a problem as you wouldn't see waves breaking on the outer edge letting you know where it was. Later, we installed satellite navigation to help, but there could be dead spots when there were no satellites available to feed you the information on your position so you still had to rely somewhat on the compass and charts. *Si Bon* also had a sixty-mile radar on board but being one hundred miles offshore the radar didn't pick up shoreline, islands, or marker buoys to help you find your position. If there was another vessel anchored out on Osprey Reef than it would show that, but it was a rare occurrence.

I met and became friends with a lot of Australian people while I lived there. I found them to never take things too seriously and always willing to have a beer or two to unwind. Once we stopped by to see a fellow out in the country who was training for the Olympics in archery. He was out back of his barn letting arrows fly when we arrived. He set down his bow for a minute and reached over for his can of Foster's beer. You must have something to steady the nerves, you know. Cheers!

STARTING OVER: AUSTRALIA

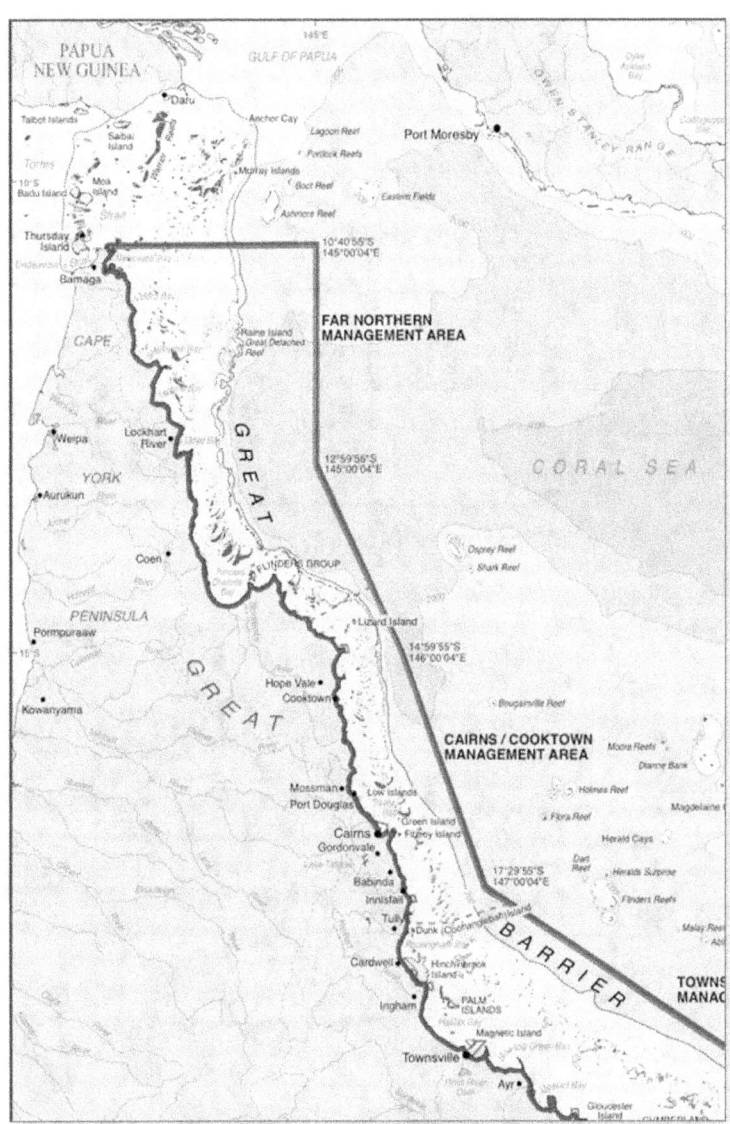

GREAT BARRIER REEF MAP

RANDOM TANGENTS

FANTASY DIVE CHARTERS

SI BON

CHAPTER ELEVEN
Aqua Time Venture: Hong Kong

After we sold Fantasy Dive Charters in 1991, I had all kinds of offers to do something different. One of the guys from a dive shop in Adelaide came up to talk to me about going over to Guam in search of a sunken treasure. His story was that there were three Spanish ships that supposedly sunk in a typhoon back in the 1600s and they carried approximately $500 million worth of gold and silver at today's values. As the supposed location of the ship was close to the Marianna Trench, I knew that we would most likely be unable to find anything there. I wished him all the luck in world! Later I heard that he had found some backers from the U.S., but I'm not sure what happened to the venture in the end.

As the final payment was made for the business I headed back to the U.S. to spend time with my children and family. Even though I had gone back every six months, this time I could stay a little longer as there was no pressure to get back quickly. Suzanne was adjusting to a little less hectic life and was spending more time with her family while I took the trip back.

Shortly after returning to Australia I decided to take my wife on a honeymoon as we hadn't done much traveling together. We moved out of the house we had rented, and off we went. First stop was Darwin, Australia, as I had never been to the north coast. From there we went up to Bali for a few days before going to Bangkok. We stayed in Bangkok for a week. We rented a car, a driver, and an interpreter to take in the sights. Since I had been there before, I was familiar with the things to see and having your own driver and interpreter was a plus. One day we went by boat to the floating market where they have boats full of produce and flowers all in one area. As we exited the boat at the wharf there was all kinds of Thai food on display that you could purchase, and I turned around and asked her.

"Suzanne, would you like to try some of the Thai food on display here?"

"Are you kidding me, I am not trying anything that I can't identify."

"You are not a very adventurous soul, are you?"

She just looked at me and I knew that was the end of the conversation as I laughed.

We had been there almost a week touring the temples, silk merchants, and gold stores. We were getting ready to leave the next day, but we found out they were having a yearly festival on the river with fireworks, so we decided to stay an extra day. The festival was called the Loy Krathong, during which they release floating baskets of flowers with candles onto the river. It was a ceremony to release one's sins. The thousands of baskets floating down the river at night were spectacular along with all the fireworks. They offered a special buffet at the hotel, which overlooked the river, so we could see everything that night.

The next day we flew to Hong Kong, where I had booked a room at the prestigious Peninsula Hong Kong Hotel for two nights as a special treat for my wife. I felt this was my opportunity to show my wife my appreciation for all the help and sacrifice she had provided while we had the diving business.

We knew a couple that lived on Hong Kong Island as they had gone on a diving trip on *Si Bon* and we were hoping to meet up with them while we were there. They were both owners of investment firms in Hong Kong at the time and were doing quite well. After we arrived, I contacted them, and the husband suggested meeting at the pier on Saturday morning. He had recently received delivery of his new fifty-five-foot Cheoy Lee fiberglass cruiser and wanted us to go out with them for the day. We met him and his wife along with several other guests at the pier on Saturday morning as his crew motored the vessel up to the dock. We cruised around the islands close to Hong Kong and stopped for lunch. We were invited to go water skiing as he also had a ski boat he towed behind his cruiser. It was a beautiful day and we enjoyed ourselves.

After coming back ashore that evening, my wife was acting a little funny and I questioned her.

"Suzanne, what is the problem? You seem distraught about something."

"The other lady on the boat today was a psychic and she started telling me things about us. I just want a ticket back home."

"What are you talking about? What did she say that has you so upset?"

"She said that you really didn't love or care for me."

"Suzanne, if I didn't love you or care for you why would I bring you on this wonderful trip to thank you for being a part of my life?"

"She said it was going to end in the future, so I just want to go home. I don't want to talk about it anymore."

RANDOM TANGENTS

"If that is really what you think and what you want, then your wish is my command."

I left her at our room in the hotel and went to see if I could find a travel agent where I could buy a ticket. I was upset that she would believe everything she was told by the psychic. It was already late at night as I walked around Hong Kong looking for a ticket agent, but they were all closed, and it was a good thing they were.

I saw an old familiar sign that said Kangaroo Pub, so I thought I would stop in and have a few beers and think about my situation. As I sat down at the bar I noticed that there were a lot of young American guys setting around it. I asked where they were all from and they responded by telling me they were sailors off the *USS Enterprise*, which had just docked. I learned that there are over 4,500 sailors on the *Enterprise* and found out the two sailors sitting on opposite sides of the bar didn't even know each other. The ship was like a small city with many levels so it made sense. I was having a good time with these young guys drinking beer and telling stories when I felt a presence behind me. It was my wife. She had found me! The sign saying "Kangaroo Pub" might have helped her a bit as I had once told her about it. She was smiling and I asked her if she wanted a drink and the prior intense talk we had seemed to have dissipated, which was a huge relief.

The next night I made reservations at an exclusive restaurant overlooking the harbor. All the waiters were men and the service was impeccable. At the end of the meal they came around with a little wooden cart that had rare bottles of French Cognac and Armagnac brandy on it. Some of dates on the bottles were from the 1920s with prices to match.

AQUA TIME VENTURE: HONG KONG

While sitting there enjoying the view across the harbor, we noticed three fellows having dinner across the room from us. They were enjoying themselves and had asked for cigars. Two girls appeared in what looked like Playboy bunny costumes with a selection of cigars on a wooden tray. After each man chose a cigar, one of the girls would pull the cigar up between her breasts and then kiss it, massage it, and cut off the end before lighting it up and handing it to the customer. It was supposed to be erotic, but my wife and I were laughing watching the show. These guys loved every bit of it, and I am sure they tipped the girls accordingly.

A couple of days later we flew to Vancouver and checked into our hotel. We rented a car for an afternoon to drive around. It was a beautiful town with flowers blooming everywhere and manicured yards along the waterfront. In the evening we explored "Gastown," the historic district with the Steam Clock. Next we caught a ferry to Victoria for the next leg of our journey and stayed at the charming Empress Hotel. The hotel sat across from the waterfront, so we spent some time just looking at the boats and inhaling the clean, crisp ocean air.

We arrived in Seattle a couple of days later on the ferry from Victoria and spent three wonderful days there exploring Pike's Place Market, doing the underground tour, and going to the top of the Space Needle. They say it rains a lot in Seattle, but we were lucky and had exceptional weather. Next we were headed to Denver and wanted to see some country, so I booked a trip on the train running to Denver from Seattle with our own sleeper compartment. Our journey took us through the beautiful Rocky Mountains.

I introduced my family to Suzanne, and we stayed in Denver for about a week. My family quickly became friends with Suzanne and loved her Australian accent and energy. Suzanne had lived in New York at one time and loved the United States. We purchased a car in Denver and went down to Santa Fe, New Mexico, where we leased an apartment for twelve months. I chose Santa Fe to show her the southwest and a totally different lifestyle. She loved the area and she could go back to Australia whenever she wished. Later we had my children down for a couple of weeks. It was all good!

I started putting together a new business plan that incorporated building two types of large scuba diving ships that would travel together all over the Pacific. The difference in the ships was that one would have a decompression chamber on board in case we ever needed it. This vessel was going to be a slightly larger ship at 132 feet while the other was to be 120 feet. I was getting an estimate for building them in Houma, Louisiana, at a shipyard that a marine architect recommended.

It took me about eight months to put together the business plan for this venture. The plan was to build two different pairs of ships so we could offer anyone booking a choice of one of two locations. This meant building two ships with recompression chambers and two smaller ships without chambers. It took a lot of time putting a schedule together; it was a logistical nightmare! Once that was completed, along with the ship designs, I put together a brochure for marketing purposes. I hired a company in California to do some test marketing to see if this concept would fly. We would sell a five-year timeshare in the venture and each share would allow you ten days a year on one of the ships. Additional days could be purchased if there was availability. The market research company came back with positive results, which indicated that the idea could turn into a viable business.

AQUA TIME VENTURE: HONG KONG

I put together the artwork and the brochure for the business, which was going to be based out of Hong Kong. The name of the venture was Aqua Time and the logo was a dolphin jumping out of the water through a rainbow. I also had a commercial artist work on pictures depicting the two styles of ships we were going to build so that they looked realistic for marketing.

As I was putting the final pricing together, I flew to Singapore to obtain pricing on building the ships there as it would be much closer to where I was going to start using them. The cost of transporting these vessels across the Pacific from New Orleans was significant. I met with a marine architect in Singapore, and he put me in touch with several ship building firms in Singapore and Australia to secure competitive pricing.

Now the only thing I had to do was find $15 million (in 1992 dollars) to put this thing together. I figured that I would make some money once I sold all the shares and a lot of the money would go toward taking care of the expenses over a five-year period. At the end of the five years, the boats would be paid off, at which time I could sell them and realize the bigger profit. At least that was the plan.

I started researching investment capital and saw an advertisement in the *New York Times* saying that a company was looking to fund projects with good business plans. I called the contact number and was put in touch with a guy in Vancouver who asked for a copy of my business plan. After *supposedly* reading it, he got back to me and said he loved it and asked if I wanted to go forward with the funding. I was overjoyed. He said it was being financed out of Switzerland, so I had to set up an offshore corporation to transfer the money. It would

RANDOM TANGENTS

cost me $20,000 to set up the corporation and provide all the paperwork for the investment.

He said once I paid the money, I would go to Switzerland to receive the funding from a Basel-based company called Globus Finance. This almost sounded too good to be true. I told him I could come up to Vancouver with cash money and he said that would expedite the process. I grabbed $20,000 in cash, taped it to myself, and flew to Vancouver. When I met this fellow, I took out the cash, reaffirmed the deal, and asked for paperwork to show exactly where the money would go and when I was going to get the funding. He came up with some paperwork and said he would get back to me shortly to give me a date to be in Basel to finish the transaction.

Before I left, he asked me a question that seemed to be a little odd.

"What would you have done if I had tried to take the cash money from you when you arrived?"

"Listen, I am ex-Army and served time in Vietnam so I would have probably just ripped your throat out. This had better be a real deal or I will be back."

He just stared at me and didn't know what to say. Sometimes you have to put a little bluff in the conversation to let them know you are serious. And why would someone ask stupid questions like that anyway? In a few days I received a message from him telling me to be in Basel in two weeks.

I booked my plane ticket to Switzerland and stopped briefly in Singapore to talk to the naval architect and give him an update on the project. As soon as I got to Basel, I went to the Globus Finance Office. I believed they were going to furnish accommodations until the financing was completed. However, at the office they acted as if they didn't know anything about

AQUA TIME VENTURE: HONG KONG

that. They told me to find a place on my own or join their other clients who were staying at a nearby hotel. I was told to check back the next day to find out when the first tranche of the financing package would be completed.

I went to find the hotel nearby and checked in. Once there, I met other people that were also waiting for financing from Globus. I found out that some had been there for as long as thirty days. One couple mortgaged their house to pay this company their upfront fee and to fly over here. Now they were getting concerned as they were quickly running out of money.

I became friends with another fellow, Larry, who told me some stories about Globus Finance. It seemed that they would come up with an excuse every couple of days as to why they could not fund anyone that day. In fact, he didn't know anyone who had been funded and some people had been there for several weeks. I was coming to the realization that this whole thing was an elaborate scam. Then I had an idea and asked him how the manager of this company was getting the money. He said that a FedEx delivery came every day and dropped off envelopes to his office and then he would go to the bank and deposit the money.

As we continued to talk, we found out that we were born on the same day and year within 120 miles of each other. Also, we both went to Southern Illinois University; he went to the Edwardsville campus and I went to Carbondale. It was phenomenal that we would meet like this. He said his wife, Karen, was an astrologer and physic and he would have to call her and tell her all about this.

After being there two days, I met with Larry.

RANDOM TANGENTS

"Larry, I want to get my money back and we just can't confront this guy in his office or else it could turn into a no-win circus."

"How would you go about getting the money back?"

"Let's wait in the garage until he comes down with the envelopes to go to the bank to make a deposit and pressure him into refunding our money."

"Do you think that will work?"

"I think it will as he doesn't want the police to get wind of the scam he is running."

"Okay, let's talk later as I wish to talk to my wife about this."

Larry called his wife and told her what I wanted to do, and she told him to listen to me. She explained to him that if we went to the authorities during the Mercury retrograde period we were in, we might not get our money back for years. Larry told me about the conversation he had with his wife later that day and I asked what she meant by a Mercury retrograde; he explained that it had to do with astrology. It was settled then: we would meet this guy the next day and obtain our refund.

The next morning, I was sitting at a table in the restaurant of the hotel having coffee and putting together a plan on paper on how we were going to pull this off. I had questions I needed answered from Larry about the approximate time when the FedEx delivery arrived and how soon afterwards did this guy come down to go to the bank. I also needed to know what he drove so that we could be close to his automobile when we approached him. When Larry appeared and sat down at my table, I started to ask him the questions I needed answers to and he stopped me. He said he had gone to the police inspector the evening before because he got worried and told the whole story to the police. He said that at that very moment the police were raiding the guy's office and taking him into custody. It was ten years before we received any money back, and even then it was only about 60 percent of the original sum. Larry should have listened to his wife!

When I returned to the U.S., I was running low on funds. I called the guy in Vancouver, knowing he kept $2,500 of the initial $20,000 I had paid as his part of the deal. First, he said he couldn't give me anything back. I told him he had better send me the money or I was coming up to Vancouver. I asked him if he remembered what I had told him I would do if he tried to take the money from me. He said he was recording the phone call and asked if I was threatening him. I said it wasn't a threat but a promise. He thought about it and sent the money back to me. It was a bluff, but it worked.

Back to the Drawing Board

I stopped in Denver to visit with my dad who was enjoying retirement and my mother who was running her used bookstore in Englewood. Mother needed something to do and she enjoyed meeting and being around people. I brought my children over for the weekend and we had a Sunday cookout to spend time together. By this time my children were twelve and fourteen years old and we could never get in enough hugs. My mother always made special desserts for my children and they loved it.

Suzanne was back in Australia spending time with her son and family when I arrived back in Santa Fe. I needed to focus on finding other funding avenues for the Aqua Time venture. I sent my business plan out to several large shipping building firms I thought would be interested in funding this project. I even took a trip to Japan to see if I might be able to find funding there as the Japanese interest in diving was growing rapidly.

I did have an interesting time while in Tokyo, though. I happened to meet a well-known underwater photographer and we went out to dinner together. He didn't speak much English, but his wife was an airline stewardess and spoke fluent English. They said they would pick me up and we would meet some of their friends at a restaurant close to the sumo wrestling arena. They told me that sumo wrestlers often ate there too. As we stepped into the restaurant, we had to take off our shoes and put them in an individual locker that you locked with a hand-carved wooden key. I thought that was neat and intricate.

We went upstairs to a room where low tables were set with cushions around them. I took off my dinner jacket and sat cross-legged on the cushion next to the table. I think my Japanese host was surprised to see an American, a *gaijin*, sit so comfortably. Everyone ordered drinks and I quickly learned that if I finished my glass of beer, the person next to me took the large bottle of beer sitting there and refilled my glass. I did the same for them; I guessed it was a way to be polite.

I let my hosts order for me. The food was brought out on plates and there was a huge metal bowl at the end of the table with a small burner under it. They poured some broth into the bowl and then added some of the food off the plates so that it could cook. When the food was done, we passed our plates around and one person at the end acted as the server. The food was memorable in a good way.

We started chatting, and I mentioned their famous Japanese swordsman, Miyamoto Musashi, and his book *The Book of Five Rings*. This book is from 1640 and is still studied by most businessmen in Japan as a guide to character and strategy. While in Australia, I read the 1,200-page biography of Miyamoto Musashi who was considered a philosopher, strategist, and a *ronin* (or masterless samurai). He served no feudal lord nor received a stipend for income. He is considered the best swordsman ever with an undefeated record of sixty-one duels. One of his last duels was with one of the best swordsmen at that time and an antagonist who wanted this duel for some time. Musashi defeated him with a boat oar that he had carved into a rough shape of a sword as he was rowed across a lake to the duel. It seems that in his haste of getting to the island for the duel he had forgotten his sword and it was too late to turn back to get it. What I learned from reading about him was that he would become totally focused on whatever he was studying, and time didn't seem to be relevant to him. He traveled the country and stopped numerous times to perfect his skills in calligraphy, writing, strategy, and even design. He once stopped at a village that was continually getting flooded by a river ruining their crops. He observed their situation for some time and then designed a terraced crop land and a water diversion to control the river. He spent some time working with them to achieve the goal and make it reality. The group I was with were impressed that I knew so much about him and the culture at that time. It was a delightful evening and I learned a lot from them and their culture today.

 Also while in Tokyo, I found a place called the 77 Sunset Strip Bar, which was a local hangout for expats. The place was packed, and I soon met a couple of ladies from the Virgin Islands who were in Tokyo working as models. I asked them why Tokyo and they said it was much easier to get into modelling in Tokyo. I also met a Canadian lady who was formerly an airline stewardess but now taught English at a school in

RANDOM TANGENTS

Tokyo. She said that quite a few English-speaking people from other countries were teaching English classes in Japan, which was interesting. I guess it would be a way to travel and make money at the same time. It was a fun evening—meeting people and finding out why they were there and what they thought of Japan.

When I returned to the U.S., I decided it was time to get back to work. I had spent a lot of time searching in many different directions for funding to no avail, so it was time to move on. I kept the business plans and some of the drawings as reminders of a past venture. It is funny how things that happen in life sometimes just seem to keep pushing you in a different direction. If you could only figure out the direction ahead of time, you could save valuable time in getting to the finish line but probably forego the many experiences you would have gained. As far as reaching the finish line maybe it is best to reach the end in a roundabout way and enjoy the ride. It seemed that even though I gave 100 percent of myself to a venture sometimes it still doesn't pan out. I learned and experienced much in the meantime. Isn't that what life is about? Experiencing it to the fullest? If you always had it easy with everything being given to you, how would you savor the lows and the highs? How could you know the emotions felt by others, in their losses and triumphs, without having a similar experience yourself? Triumphs and losses are the spices in life and hopefully when the time comes for you to leave this place you will look at your life as one big picture show that you created and that you leave with a smile on your face knowing that the journey was worth the price.

CHAPTER TWELVE
The Hunt Begins

I contacted the fellow I met in Basel, Larry, who lived in Sedona, Arizona, with his wife, Karen. As I was talking to him over the phone, he started telling me about a guy who had a 20,000-acre ranch about sixty miles south of Douglas, Arizona, in Mexico. He said that during the Great Depression, which lasted from 1929 until 1939, there had been some gold mining on this ranch. It seemed that Mexican placer miners called *gambusinos* had found enough gold nuggets to survive the Great Depression and there were tales of a lot more there. Placer mining involves taking gravel in and along a streambed and processing it in hopes of finding gold. He said he could introduce me to one of the owners of the ranch and maybe we could do a little exploration. He was primarily interested in the zeolite that was on the property as it could be used for a lot of different types of filtration. This sounded like a great adventure!

Suzanne had come back from Australia shortly after I had moved us out of the Santa Fe property, so I asked her if she wanted to go prospecting for a while in Mexico. My father had a van fitted with bunk beds, a stove, and a fridge along with an all-terrain vehicle (ATV) on a trailer that we could pull behind the van. Suzanne was all in for the adventure, so we packed the van with food, clothes, metal detectors, a small mining dredge, tools, and gold pans, and set off to Arizona. We met up with one of the owners of the ranch and Larry. The deal was that we would split any of the gold that we found.

We crossed the border into Mexico and the Mexican customs guy checked our passports and waved us through. We hadn't gone one hundred feet when another customs guy started waving at us to stop. He came to the front door of the van where my wife was standing. She automatically invited him inside to look if he wanted to, but he backed away and waved us on. I think he was surprised that my wife just motioned him in, and he didn't know what to do. In hindsight, I figure he wanted a small bribe to let us continue.

We arrived at the ranch later in the afternoon. The owner went over the map I had of the area and pointed out certain areas on it they had prospected before; it was a start. We found a place to camp out alongside a nice stream with a gravel bed and lined with sycamore trees. The water was crystal clear in the stream and was fairly warm. We had brought a little three-inch dredge along so we could dredge for gold in the stream beds. I used it to suck out a hole in the streambed, so we had a place to jump in and cool off. We stayed there for six weeks as I walked all over the mountains on the ranch and explored where the Mexican gambusinos used dry rockers for finding the gold. A dry rocker was a table made with a metal top with holes in it which allowed certain size rocks to fall through as they rocked it. The bottom of the table looked like wooden curved rockers off a rocking chair. Sometimes these dry rockers would have two or three levels of metal sheets with smaller holes in them as the material fell through from the top—dividing the material into different gradations. This helped them in seeing gold in the material and made it easier for them to take the material,

THE HUNT BEGINS

add water, and pan it to find gold. After close investigation of the area I determined that for an operation to be economically viable, one would have to bring in some big equipment and move a lot of material to process it for the gold. It didn't look like a viable option as sufficient water for the processing was unavailable.

One night after we had set up camp, I was going through the little closet in the back of the van to see what we had packed. Standing in a corner covered with some bedding and blankets was a rifle.

"Suzanne, why is there a rifle hidden in the closet?"

"Well, I was telling your father that I was afraid of mountain lions and bears, so he put the rifle there."

"Do you know it is illegal to bring guns across the border?"

"But your father thought I needed protection."

"They put people in prison for this! I could be spending ten years in a Mexican prison! I wish you had told me."

"What are we going to do with it now?"

"Just keep it hidden in the closet. I don't worry about going back across the border into the United States. I would have hated to be eating beans and tortillas for ten years though!"

She started laughing. "You know I would have come to visit you, right?"

The ranch house used on the property used to have a large hacienda that an English couple lived in back in the early 1900s. He supposedly had some sort of English title and was managing this large property for raising cattle, cutting timber, and mining. The wife was helping the locals with education and whatever else she could; she was revered by the Mexican people who lived in the area. When she died, she was buried on the ranch under a big oak tree. Her grave can still be found at the ranch with a fence around it to keep the cattle out. The story goes that after the English fellow left to go back to England, General Diaz came through and burned down the large hacienda and left only the outbuildings standing.

When my wife and I went over to that side of the ranch, we met the other owner, who was the brother of the first guy we met. This brother owned 6,000 acres of the 20,000 acres. His part was where the hacienda had stood, and had a stream running through it so it was more valuable. This brother went to school in Arizona and got an electrical engineering degree and met his wife while working in California. She was Italian, spoke fluent Spanish, and said the she had started the first Spanish newspaper in California. When his father died, they decided they had better move back to Mexico and take care of the ranch before it was destroyed over time. They repaired two of the large adobe buildings that remained and made them into living accommodations—one for themselves and the other one for the cowboys they hired to herd their cattle and mend the fences. There was one smaller outbuilding they called the icehouse. It was a double-walled adobe building, which provided a good thermal barrier to the weather during the summer or winter. They cut ice during the winter from the ponds and stored it here for the summer, covered with sawdust and wood chips to keep it from melting.

We became pretty good friends with this couple and their two young boys, and they invited us over for Thanksgiving dinner in the fall of 1993. The night before Thanksgiving, as we were preparing to call it a night at our camp, there were a lot of gunshots down along the stream not far from where we were camped. I wondered what the heck was going on and thought it best to stay put. The next day we went over for dinner, and

THE HUNT BEGINS

she had baked two wild turkeys in chili sauce; it was delicious. The wild turkeys had all dark meat and were much tastier than store bought ones. She told us that they had offered two local Mexican boys a pair of Levi's each if they brought back two turkeys for their Thanksgiving dinner. So that was the reason for all the shooting. As for the number of shots fired, they should have had fifty turkeys. It sounded like a war zone!

While hiking every day, I would take the same path and head toward the mountains. One day I found a turkey feather on the path and picked it up and left a coin in its place. Why did I leave the coin? Well, there is an old saying that if you take something from the wild, you should leave something in its place. I thought if I could find another feather, I would have one for each of my children. The next day, another feather appeared on my path and I left a coin again. When I started out the next day, I thought to myself that I would like to have one for myself. Well, there was one on my path again! I never wished for another feather to appear and didn't see another one on my path for the remainder of my time there. Was this all pure coincidence?

While hiking through the mountains on the ranch, I had a metal detector with me and every so often I would turn it on if I thought there could be some gold in the ground or in a stream. One day I found a black seam in the rock and turned my detector on, and it went off. I picked up a few pieces of this black rock and took it with me. When I showed it to the first brother, he said it was nothing and threw the piece on the ground. I didn't say a word, but it was some pretty high-grade silver. This brother, I heard, had let drug dealers land their plane on the property at one time, so I questioned his trustworthiness. At this time, I thought it best not to say anything more as I didn't want to cause problems between brothers.

    Before going to the ranch, I purchased a couple of topographical maps of the area so that I would have a good perspective of all the mountains and streams on their property. I sent an identical topo map to two different people who advertised map dowsing, one in Texas and the other in Arizona. Map dowsing is done by swinging a pendulum over a map to locate what you are looking for. This is much like water witching or dowsing except you are doing it over a map versus walking over an area with a dowsing rod in your hands. I wanted to see if what they would come back with, after they dowsed the maps, was close to what I knew of the area. I was even hoping that I would learn a little more. They both sent back their findings after a couple of weeks and both said the ranch had large amounts of silver and only small amounts of gold. The map dowser in Arizona said that there was also a diamond chimney not far away and some rich gold deposits on the other side of the mountain. I knew about the rich gold deposits on the other side of the mountain but not the diamond chimney. When it comes to dowsing there are many skeptics saying it is all baloney and unscientific. I just take a stand back approach and if it works fine and if it doesn't then no big deal. I believe a few people have the gift and many others don't.

    When Suzanne and I left after six weeks, having found no gold, we headed back to Colorado to see my parents and return the camper van and ATV. It was a great adventure and I must hand it to Suzanne for camping out for six weeks with few conveniences. When we got back to Colorado, we unloaded everything, then we went down to see my mother. At sixty-five years old, she had started a small used bookstore in Englewood,

Colorado, and had a lot of children's books. We boxed up some and sent them to the ranch in Mexico for those young boys. Their mother was delighted to have new reading material for the boys as she homeschooled them.

Metaphysics in My Life

Soon after Suzanne flew back to Australia to spend some more time with her family, I met up with a friend named Carelyn, my old travel agent, who had become a mentor to me in exploring metaphysics. She was well read and traveled, and I enjoyed hearing some of the adventures that she had been involved in. One day she told me that I was not my body and I was not my mind, which struck me as odd. What did she mean by that? It took me a couple of years to put the pieces together for the puzzle and to open my mind to a different way of thinking.

What I came to realize was that if you live entirely on the physical plane, you are tied into your body and your mind, which are mostly controlled by the ego. By this I mean the emotion that you experience gives you the feeling of being a person who you see in the mirror and those emotions are what makes you human. Those emotions control how you interact with the world and how you view the world. The ego is the main proponent that controls your emotions and you. But if you are on the spiritual plane, you see things differently and don't let your emotions go untethered while facing the everyday dramas and superficial problems. This is when you realize who you are—a pure spirit acting out a scene on planet earth. The life you are witnessing is like a light shining through a celluloid film onto a screen. What makes it feel real is the emotion that you inject into the scenes that you experience. To be or not to be, that is the question? The only problem I find with this is being able to lift yourself up to that higher spiritual level all the time. You may only get a brief glimpse occasionally as you travel through life and search for the truth. Everyone has their beliefs; these are only my way of looking at things.

Carelyn used to do psychometry, which was a way of giving psychic readings to people. She would take a personal item from a person, hold it, and then tell them what she saw. She said she had quit doing that because many of the people she thought were friends only wanted her for a reading. I had never asked her, but now that we met up again, she asked me to give her something that was personal to me, so I gave her my watch. She held it with her eyes closed for a minute and started laughing. She said, "You were an ugly Indian in your past life. I see you kneeling by a stream in the sunlight and people seeking you out to help them. You were a shaman to the tribe." Very interesting!

She told me about a physic center in Denver that gave readings, so I made an appointment there to get a past life reading done just for fun. Life is about opening up to new things and possibilities so I thought that would be a unique experience. It was just another spice to try in the journey through life. The young lady that did the reading had a degree in psychology and was also part Native American from a tribe in the northeastern United States. She put me in a sort of hypnotic trance and started asking me questions about my past lives. She recorded it so that I could listen to all the questions and answers from the session afterwards. After each question, she would snap her finger next to my ear and the answer would just pop into my brain. It was amazing!

THE HUNT BEGINS

What came out of the session was that I was once a doctor in England, my wife died young, and we had two children. Those two children are the same two children who I have today in spirit. My next life was that of a Native American shaman in Arizona. Even my name was revealed, which meant "light in the stream." That struck a chord as Carelyn had also seen me as a shaman, kneeling by a stream. My brother at that time was my father today and my sister then was my Australian wife. To believe all of this, one must believe in reincarnation—that we keep coming back to earth in spirit but in a different body. As the answers just seemed to pop into my head, I couldn't say where they came from. One might think they were hallucinations even though I hadn't done any drugs. This was a different kind of experience for sure.

She also said I was very close to hawks and told me how to say hello to them in the Native American language. From then on, I have always said hello to my hawk brothers whenever I see them. They always seem to know when I am around and appear. Once, while driving from Missouri back to Denver with my brother, I counted fifty-two hawks along the way. One even flew right at my windshield then veered off. This special relationship has helped me connect more and more with nature as I watch for hawks and listen for the call of the ravens in the wind.

New Directions

I looked for some work around Denver and found a job selling insurance to self-employed people. I thought this would be a good way to make some dollars, so I studied and took the test to get my insurance license. The company I started working for

RANDOM TANGENTS

gave me all the leads they had for southern Colorado, and I was happy to have an area to myself. Little did I know that this part of Colorado is very depressed, and the average income is low. What I was selling insurance for to a whole family was more than their monthly house payments. These people couldn't pay these rates on the income they had. My insurance salesman days were short-lived.

It was late spring of 1994 and Suzanne had decided to stay in Australia to be around her son and family more. I needed to seriously start making some money and I knew one thing well—construction. I sold my car, bought a truck, and headed to Mesa, Arizona, to work on a water treatment plant. During this time, I stayed in contact with Larry, so I stopped in Sedona on my way to Mesa to meet up with him and Karen to get to know each other a little better.

As an astrologer Karen could tell a lot about you just by your birth date, but she was also a psychic. When I went to downtown Sedona with her, she walked up to a lady and asked her about her liver problem without even knowing her. The lady conceded that she had a problem, and Karen told her she needed to take care of it quickly. How did she know this?

Just before leaving, Karen gave me a "gambling time," a twenty-minute window that was coming up in two days, which could prove to be lucky if I wanted to gamble. I left Sedona and traveled south to Cottonwood and spent some time at the old mining town called Jerome. From there I traveled over to Camp Verde and east to the top of the Mogollon Rim and then down to Payson. I stopped for breakfast at an Indian casino as the gambling time she gave me was coming up. I waited until after breakfast and went over to a slot machine and in three

THE HUNT BEGINS

pulls I hit the jackpot. I walked out with a handful of $100 bills that I needed. Karen's abilities were remarkable!

While visiting them in Sedona, Larry mentioned that he had met an old guy named John living up in Strawberry, Arizona, who swore he knew where the Lost Dutchman's Gold Mine was. The Lost Dutchman, one of the most famous lost gold mines, is located somewhere in the Superstition Mountains outside of Apache Junction, Arizona. He gave me John's phone number so I could contact him later. This was the start of another tangent in an unplanned life.

CHAPTER THIRTEEN
Lost Dutchman Mine

I started working on a water treatment plant located in Mesa, not far from Phoenix, and camped out in the desert most of the time close to Apache Junction (it didn't cost anything). I could catch a shower at a national fitness chain that I had a membership to, and weekends were pretty much free. Being close to the Superstition Mountains, I was intrigued by the story of the Lost Dutchman's Gold Mine. I spent my spare time reading up on the treasure story.

Shortly after I started working in Mesa, I contacted John by phone. I told him that I would like to hear the story he had about the Lost Dutchman. We decided to meet the following weekend at his home in Strawberry. He was about eighty years old at the time and was getting around his house with the help of a walker.

We talked for a while and he told me a lot about his life. He was a civil engineer before he retired. He said he was always looking for treasures and had accumulated stories and maps over the years. His father was a miner and a surveyor back around 1900, and John was born at a small mining camp close to Nipton, California. As a child he played with the Indian children who lived close by and even spoke some of their language.

When he was a child, he caught pneumonia. As penicillin hadn't been discovered yet, the Indians gave his father something that looked like a weed and told him to boil it up as a tea. He drank it in the evening and by the next morning his chest was clear, he could breathe, and he was ready to go play again. He remembered what the weed looked like and over the years he had gone back several times to the New York Mountains in California to replenish his stash. He said he usually found the bushy plant growing at about the 6,000-foot elevation. He showed it to me, and it looked like a small four-leaf clover on the end of a stem.

John said he had to use it a couple of times over the years. Once, not that long ago, while he was in the hospital, he came down with pneumonia and the doctors had given up on him. He called his caregiver at the time and told her to find a brown paper bag with this particular weed in his closet. He told her to bring a quart jar of it boiled up as a tea to him. By the next morning, the pneumonia was gone, and the doctors couldn't believe it. They kept him another day running tests to see what had happened. John said he never told the doctors his secret.

John said that he tried for some time to make a medicine out of the weed by using alcohol and other means to extract the medicinal properties but didn't succeed. He said he took some of the weed to a pharmacy a long time ago telling the pharmacist what it was used for and the pharmacist pointed to a row of jars on his top shelf that were filled with different plants for different ailments. The pharmacist said they were are all good natural cures, but people don't want to take the time to prepare them, they just want to take a pill and go on.

Another story John told about the healing properties of herbs and plants was about an older lady who had arthritis. It seemed her fingers had become so curled up she couldn't hold her darning needles any more to knit. John gathered some

RANDOM TANGENTS

leaves and twigs off some creosote bushes and put them into a crock pot and let them stew for a few hours. He told this lady to soak her hands in the liquid a couple of times a day as hot as she could stand it. He also told her to make a new batch once a week and to get rid of the old. When he stopped back by in a couple of months she was sitting on her front porch knitting away. Her fingers were almost straight and she said the pain had mostly gone away. Another old-time remedy that has been forgotten.

After we talked for a while, John got an old map and told me what he knew about the Lost Dutchman's Mine. I came to find out that over the past century, many people have died and disappeared looking for the mine in the Superstition Mountains. As John told the story, I took notes and looked closely at his map to make sure I understood everything.

The story revolves around a miner named Jacob Waltz and a gold mine that he had back in the Superstition Mountains that once belonged to a Spanish family named Peralta. Waltz had become friends with one of the Peralta heirs and was allegedly told about the mine in the Superstition Mountains. In about 1877, Waltz took a partner named Weiser to help him mine. Later, Weiser disappeared while Waltz was away from the mine for several days. When Waltz returned Weiser was nowhere to be found. Waltz believed the Indians had ambushed and killed him while others believed that Waltz had killed him. After that, Waltz was careful when he went back into the mountains as men would try to follow him to find out where the mine was. He brought out some rich gold ore when he came out of the mountains but would never file a claim on the mine as he didn't want anyone to know where it was. He knew if they found it, they would probably kill him to take it; he was cautious. In the end Waltz was caught in a flash flood at his homestead along the Superstitions and was saved by two brothers. He was taken to town and cared for by a woman named Julia Thomas. Waltz had contracted pneumonia and his health deteriorated. In the end he tried to tell one of the brothers and Julia where the mine was and how to get to it. After he died, they spent years looking for it in vain. Waltz died in 1891 and the search continues.

John said at one time there was a little ranch called Milk Ranch located on Milk Ranch Creek just north of what is today Queen Valley. The fellow and his wife who lived there raised goats and sold milk and cheese over at the Silver King Mine. John said that one morning when the wife went outside, she saw Jacob Waltz, alias the Dutchman, at their well getting some water. She knew who he was, so she waved and went on. A lot of people had tried to follow Waltz back into the mountains to find his gold mine, but he always took a different route and gave them the slip. With this bit of information John believed the mine was actually east of Weavers Needle instead of west as many others thought it was.

John said another one of the clues to the location came from a story written about two soldiers who had accidentally found a mine in the Superstitions. They had mustered out of the Army at Ft. McDowell in either 1879 or 1880, depending on which story you read, and were walking across the Superstitions to get a job at the Silver King Mine when they stumbled upon a mine shaft. They picked up some samples to take with them. After reaching the Silver King Mine, they found out how rich in gold the ore they had picked up was, so they headed to Apache Junction to pick up supplies so they could go back and file a claim. They had documented where it was with a map but were killed shortly after they left Apache Junction.

When the bodies of the two soldiers were found, they didn't have the map on them anymore. It seemed someone must have overheard them the night before while they were at a bar in Apache Junction. The guy mopping the saloon floor, who had a club foot, was soon implicated in the crime as he was found gambling heavily in the next town. Where did he get the money from if not off the dead soldiers? The local sheriff went looking for him, but he had disappeared.

Years later a man appeared in Apache Junction asking who knew the Superstition Mountains the best. He was referred to a rancher named Jim Bark and a fellow named Sims Ely, who was the local newspaper editor. The two men had been searching for the Lost Dutchman for years. Sims Ely later wrote a book called *The Lost Dutchman Mine* about his and Jim Bark's search for the mine. It is probably one of the best written and most informative books about the story; many other books have been written but they have plenty of embellishment.

The stranger talked to Ely and asked him if he knew of a green spring located in the Superstition Mountains. Ely told him the only green spring he knew of only had green moss on it during certain times of the year. This fellow showed Ely part of a map with a green spring and a trail going over the mountain to the next mountain that had a natural bridge on it. The fellow said he got the map from a prospector in Alaska that had a club foot.

With this information John went looking and told me that he had in fact found the green spring on the east side of Hewitt Ridge across from Millsite Canyon. Green water was coming out of the rocks and then disappeared again. John said he went up almost to the top of the mountain on the west side of Millsite Canyon where the natural bridge was. There was a shelf right below the top of the mountain. On that flat area he saw a tree that seemed out of place. It was a soft material; John thought that the hole beneath it was a mine that had been filled in with dirt and rubble and that this tree was planted on top of it.

John also said he saw charcoal up against a large flat rock sticking up vertically, which also had black soot on it. His explanation of this was that during the Spanish mining period, the shaft had several smelters set up to melt the ore down into gold. They would use coke, a charcoal type material made from wood or coal, to burn at the smelters, thus producing soot on the rock. It could be a good explanation considering all the pieces to the story. Gold fever again!

I waited until I got back to Denver and asked my father if he wanted to go camping down in the Superstitions. My son happened to be out of school for the summer and I asked if he wanted to go with us. Both of them were in for a camping trip, so we loaded up my father's van and ATV and headed to Arizona.

We camped next to the mouth of Millsite Canyon as Peacock Canyon ran to the west from there. My son was fourteen years old and he hiked all over those mountains while my father stayed with his ATV exploring the canyon. We always watched for rattlesnakes when out in the mountains; the first 200 yards into Millsite Canyon was full of them. My father even bought himself knee-high leg protectors to wear as he drove his ATV. Further back into the canyon there were javelinas (wild pigs) that would kill and eat snakes if they saw them, so you didn't have to worry as much once you got into their territory. You just had to be aware that the javelina could get a little aggressive if cornered. If you heard or saw them, you stood still, and they would normally leave.

One day while climbing up a steep slope with a lot of rock rubble I reached to pull myself up to a ledge. There was a large Gila monster hissing at me! They are nasty and ugly lizards that can give you a pretty bad bite. I jumped back and down about ten feet and quickly took a detour.

We spent several days hiking into the canyon and I worked on fixing up the road enough so dad could drive his ATV all the way back to the place where we hiked up the mountain. There was a small spring called Rattlesnake Spring in the creek bed on the right side of the road, which was about two miles in from where we started. John said at one time there had been a trough built at the spring to catch water for cattle that were grazing in this area. The main geographical marker on the west side of the road and up the mountain from Rattlesnake Spring is what they call a "natural" bridge. It was a big hole, about fifteen feet in diameter, through a vertical rock outcropping at the top of the mountain. This could easily be seen once you were in there. John thought the Lost Dutchman's Mine was to one side of the natural bridge. He had also told me there was water up there in a little seep under an overhanging rock.

The last day and night we camped next to E. Hewitt Canyon Road and Queen Creek. My son played in the water most of the day as I explored with the ATV. This was where the turnoff was onto Hewitt Canyon Road that led back to Hewitt and Millsite Canyons. That evening after dinner we were sitting in a couple of lawn chairs when a black coachwhip snake came slithering thorough our campsite. He was gone in a flash; we were glad it wasn't a rattler! The next morning we headed back to Denver and called it quits for the summer. My son loved the adventure and hiking, and his grandfather always loved the time we shared together. Just before I finished the project in Mesa, my daughter also came down for a week and we spent time tubing down the Salt River and jet skiing on Canyon Lake. We always made time each summer to spend time together wherever I was.

While working my job in Mesa I had time to go out and do some more exploring on weekends. We were getting into the heat of summer, and the desert can be brutal during the day. One weekend I went back out to the canyon and thought I would hike up to the top with only one quart of water. I thought I could easily find the seep that John said was there. When I got to the top, the only water I saw was in the hole where the tree had been rooted, and it was dirty. I started searching for the seep. After looking for a while climbing around rocks, my tongue was starting to swell up. I needed water, so I drank from the dirty water and took some in my canteen to make sure I could make it back down to the bottom. Lesson learned!

A couple of weeks later I went back up to the top again, this time with plenty of water, and finally found the seep hidden behind some bushes under an overhanging rock. There was a little basin of water covered in green moss that the seep dripped into. I found a couple of pieces of pottery shards, so I imagined the Indians knew of it many years ago. Also on the rock wall under the overhang were initials carved by John and some of his crew as their testimony that they had been there.

My next job was a water treatment plant in Henderson, Nevada, and I worked on it through late summer and well into the fall of 1994. On some weekends I would head back to Arizona, talk with John, listen to some more of his treasure stories, and gather more information and maps. I contacted

RANDOM TANGENTS

my father and my brother Jim, who was also into mining, to get together and go back up into the Superstitions to see if we could open up the shaft or find a vein structure that showed gold. They were both in for the adventure, so I started planning.

I went to the Forest Service in Phoenix to see what permit I would need. The Superstition Wilderness area was close to where we wanted to open the shaft, so I had to do some research to find the exact description and to determine the boundary. The documents stated that the boundary was the "hydrographic divide," which meant that if water flowed off the ridge one way, it was Forest Service land, and if it flowed the other way, it was Superstition Wilderness. I had to be precise in mapping out the area we were going to be working in to make sure we weren't in the wilderness area.

After climbing back up to the site, I could tell that the shaft we wished to open was about ten feet inside the wilderness area so we would just have to open another shaft up on the same vein structure inside the Forest Service land. I mapped it all out designating where we would be camped and where we would be working, then applied for a permit.

My brother and father kicked in a few dollars and I lined up all the necessary equipment. When he arrived in Arizona, my father was staying at his sister's house in Mesa, where he fell sick. He was eighty then and they put him in the hospital for a few days to run some tests.

My brother and I had a helicopter lift all our equipment up to where we would be camping. I had left a white cross marker on the landing spot so the pilot could find it. The helicopter couldn't lift too much weight at one time, so I had 500-pound bundles made up. Within two hours we had everything on top—our tents, generator, drills, drinking water, food, and explosives that we would need to open up a shaft.

In those days, you could buy ammonia nitrate sticks and mixing fluid to make explosives for mining as long as you had identification, insurance, mine location, and the haul route. You could also buy electric detonators with a fifteen-foot leg and keep them separated as an added precaution. This was to avoid all the insurance and certifications needed for hauling regular explosives such as dynamite or emulsion explosives. We also bought a spool of detonation cord to connect the blast holes. The cord is made of a plastic-type explosive and it is used for setting off all the blast holes almost simultaneously. Professionals on big projects use timers or delays on the blast holes so they have more control over the detonation.

I paid the helicopter pilot and hiked my way up to the top of the mountain to help my brother get everything set up. We were in constant communication with my father's sister, and it seemed my father's health problem was due to the fact that his medication had changed prior to coming down to Arizona; he was having a reaction to it. After we got the camp set up, I hiked back down the next day and went to Mesa to get my father out of the hospital. The hospital was running unnecessary tests and running the insurance bill up.

After getting him released, he spent the night with his sister. I wanted him to wait a couple of days before he came up, but he was adamant about getting up on the mountain, so the next day his sister and her husband drove him out to Goldfield where I had arranged for the helicopter to fly him up to our camp. The pilot thought it was a real kick that my father was going on such an adventure. When they touched down, all my father could say was how rugged the area was and how in the

RANDOM TANGENTS

hell one could get off the top of this mountain as it was sheer drop-offs all around. I think he truly enjoyed the helicopter ride; the pilot even had a headset on him as they were flying through the mountains explaining where they were.

We spent six weeks up there during February and March of 1994, and being close to the top of the mountain, we experienced some strong winds and even a little snow. In the old canvas Army tent, we had a propane stove we started in the morning to warm things up and make coffee. I often made biscuits and gravy, as we had a little electric oven, which was my father's favorite and a good high-carb breakfast that helped us get started. I had also rigged up a teepee structure and fitted it with a water bag that had a shower head on it. We would either let the sun heat the bag of water or we heated a gallon of water to pour in with the cooler water so we could have a warm shower. At 45 degrees it was pretty nippy taking a shower and it didn't take us long to get dried off in the cool air.

Once a week I would make a run to town and pick up anything that we needed. My father always seemed to have a long shopping list. This wasn't an easy task as I would have to leave early in the morning and mostly run the ridges of the mountain and down the slopes to get to my truck two hours later. I kept a clean shirt in the truck to put on as mine was always sweat soaked by the time I got there. I would then head into Apache Junction, pick up what we needed, and do a load of laundry before heading back. On the way back, I would have a full backpack. Some parts of the trail were mostly gone—close to some steep drop-offs, so you had to be especially careful as nobody would find you for days back there if something happened to you. I would make it back to camp just before dark.

LOST DUTCHMAN MINE

In 1994 we had cell phones with a battery the size of a brick and if we got on a high point on the mountain, we were able to pick up a transmitter tower and make a call. This way, we could stay in touch with family and the helicopter service if we needed them, especially since my father was getting up there in age.

Back at our camp, after about four weeks we ran out of explosives, so I took my brother to town with me to pick up another box of ammonia nitrate sticks and the mixing fuel that went with it. We left father on top as he couldn't hike out and he was fine with that. My brother was cursing me all the way out as he couldn't believe how rough the terrain was. On the way back, I put the thirty-pound box of explosives in my backpack while my brother packed some provisions (more instant gravy mix!) and up the mountain we went. This time we hiked in from Rattlesnake Springs as my brother didn't like the idea of coming back the way we went out. I thought this may be a little easier climb. At about 400 yards in when I was starting to go up the hill, a golden eagle jumped up about twenty yards in front of me and looked me straight in the eye. It was amazing as I watched him take flight. I turned around to my brother who was about twenty yards behind me and asked if he had seen the eagle. He hadn't seen anything! How was that possible?

When we got to the top of the mountain, my brother said he wouldn't do that again and that I was surely a mountain goat hopping through those mountains and brush. We unpacked the explosives and continued working until about dark when we chowed down on some rice and beans.

On one of my weekly runs into town I thought I could find a faster route if I scaled a seventy-foot cliff and got on top instead of traversing around the edge of the mountain. The cliff

RANDOM TANGENTS

had a two-foot-wide slot going all the way to the top—at least it looked that way. I figured I could wedge myself in that slot and work my way to the top with my small backpack. As I got to the top, there was a blockage that I couldn't get past. It was a tense few moments while fear started to overcome me because there was a good chance I would fall if I made a mistake. I tried to stay calm while I eased out of my pack and threw it over the top. That allowed me a little more movement and I was able to get my hands up to a higher ledge so that I could pull myself up and then on to the top. Once safely there, I asked myself why in the hell I took the chance. If I had fallen, nobody would have found me for at least a day, and I probably would have been a goner.

At the end of our six weeks up there we determined that there wasn't any gold in the area, so we cleaned everything up as we packed. I had arranged for the helicopter to come back and take us off. Altogether, it proved to be an adventure that we wouldn't soon forget. I would say that if I were going to look for the mine any further, I would draw a line between the place we were and Ft. McDowell and try to figure out how the soldiers hiked through the mountains. One would have to research old Army trails through the mountains that the two soldiers might have used. Also, they most likely stayed on high ground to avoid all the underbrush at the bottom of the canyons. Today it is mostly Superstition Wilderness area and if you do find anything you will have to turn it over to the U.S. government. However, if you do decide to have a look, it is some tough country with limited cell phone service, so you better have a companion with you. Always make sure you study the topo maps for possible water as it is a major concern back in this country especially during the hotter months. Always dress

LOST DUTCHMAN MINE

in long pants, long-sleeve cotton shirts, and gloves to protect yourself. Cacti love bare skin!

After this adventure we all headed back to Colorado to help father unpack his van that he and my brother had brought down with all the tools. I went back down to Strawberry to talk with John before I headed to Las Vegas to start another project. John had other stories and maps that he started telling me about. He could go on for hours.

The Rest of the Story

I can add a little more about this adventure now as I did some follow-up on the history of the area. The rock fence that I had come across on one of my hikes into Millsite Canyon and the old watering trough at Rattlesnake Spring were all part of a former large cattle operation. A rancher was running a large herd of cattle back in this country and was selling them to the Army. The pieces started fitting together. I even found an old mule shoe on a trail close to where we were camping out on top. Once you put this all together, it seemed likely that cowboys had actually camped out on top and had a campfire next to the vertical rock where John thought the Spanish had smelters built. The tree he dug up might have been explained by birds carrying seeds for a long distance and one took root here. John's story seemed to be a bit shaky if you did your research.

Also, if you read about the Lost Dutchman Mine, the Indians supposedly spent a couple of months covering up and erasing any signs of the mine so that white men would never find it again. The mountains were sacred to them and after running the Spanish out they didn't want another influx of miners.

RANDOM TANGENTS

Over the following years I would go in search of the different treasure stories John told me. Often I would work on several of John's stories at the same time—depending on where they were, where I was working, and the time of year. Some of the areas were not accessible in the winter. I searched for different treasures all over Arizona and California. I was even hired by two different treasure hunting groups to go after treasures they thought they knew the location of. In the end it was another period in my life in which I learned and experienced much. I loved the adventure of being out in the desert or mountains with nobody to bother you. The stars in the sky at night were amazing and made you feel how small and how lucky you really were. Ego check!

CHAPTER FOURTEEN
Heart Mountain

Sitting under my twenty-foot by forty-foot shelter out in the blazing Arizona sun, I was trying to cool off after another day of digging. I had been hired to go after a Spanish treasure that was supposedly buried close to Heart Mountain, which was in the rugged desert and mountains east of Superior, Arizona.

It was springtime of 1998 when I got the call from a group of treasure hunters who wanted to go after a Spanish treasure. The group was made up of three guys: two promoters and a money man. The story was that the treasure was buried by Jesuit priests fleeing the New Mexico territory at the time Mexico and the United States were in conflict. It was said the priests had a substantial store of gold and silver they didn't want confiscated so they buried it on their way to California. But a truth only exists once the story is proven.

The treasure hunting group had been given my name by my friends, Larry and Karen in Sedona, as they happened to know one another. Why did they need me? Well, I had mining experience, and they wanted me to sink a shaft to the treasure location. This would take equipment, explosives, and hard work, which they knew nothing about. The area where they wanted me to dig was in rough terrain on a steep slope coming down the side of the mountain. Easy access? Forget it!

RANDOM TANGENTS

My fee was $6,000 up front for supplies, $300 per foot for digging the shaft, and 10 percent of whatever we found. I never expected to find anything, so I priced my time accordingly, knowing that I could probably get one-and-a-half to two feet per day. I knew the deeper I went, the slower the pace to get the material out of the hole became. Digging straight down was dangerous work as you had to blast the material with explosives, dig it out by hand using a hoist from above, and then shore the shaft up with timber so that it didn't cave in on you.

Heart Mountain got its name from a large heart-shaped design on the side of the mountain along with a burrow and an arrow next to it. I purchased and studied all the books by Charles Kenworthy, who wrote a lot about Spanish treasures in the southwest along with markings and symbols that the Spanish used. In a picture of Heart Mountain in one of his books, it looked as though the symbols laid out on the side of the mountain were made from rocks. Kenworthy had his own interpretation of what the rocks meant; he believed the Spanish treasure was several days ride from this symbol. I could see from the picture that at one time the symbols covered the whole side of the mountain. However, when I arrived there, the heart symbol had been destroyed by treasure hunters looking for a cave entrance using a bulldozer. (They never found it.) Even then, you could still make out parts of the arrow and the burrow.

The treasure hunting group said they had flown over the area in a helicopter to determine exactly where the treasure was. They hired a fellow who claimed to have a special camera with the technology to see beneath the surface of the ground and detect objects and voids. The guy's claim to fame was that his father had been in Vietnam and used this camera to detect underground tunnels. To be honest, as long as they were paying me, I didn't care who else they hired, even though I was skeptical about this "special" camera. At least I had some free time to go and explore on my own and be out in the desert under the stars again.

Before I left Denver for Heart Mountain, I had loaded my father's ATV, a shelter, tarps, and some mining tools onto my truck. I also loaded on a cable winch my father had made for me just for this project. I would use it to pull all the material out of the shaft as I dug it out. While driving down to Arizona, I stopped in Congress, Arizona, and met up with my brother, Jim, and a friend of his for breakfast. His friend said his son, Luke, needed some work and asked if he might tag along and help me. I agreed.

At first, Luke wanted to be paid before we started, and I told him that wasn't the way the world worked. He grumbled but followed me down to Superior, Arizona. He left his pickup at a spot that the treasure hunting group had rented in Superior, and we headed to the area where I was going to build camp.

I purchased a steel-framed shelter—you basically snapped together and tightened a few bolts, a lightweight tarp for the cover, and a custom-made silver reflective cover that went on the top. I was hoping the reflective cover would help eliminate some of the heat. We put in a wooden floor in one half of the shelter and then built a small table and a shelf for our camp stove and supplies. We also built a four-foot by eight-foot-tall shower stall out of plywood. I even put up a shower curtain for a little privacy. Shower water was supplied by a five-gallon water bag with a hose and a shower head on it. It was pretty basic, but was all we needed?

RANDOM TANGENTS

The first couple of days, I noticed that Luke would go outside our tent at night and stare at the sky. One night he pointed at the stars.

"Do you see the UFOs flying around?"

I looked at the thousands of stars in the sky. "Where?"

He pointed at a bright star a little above the horizon. "The bright one right there. If you stand and watch it for a while, it moves across the sky."

I stood and watched for a couple of minutes as he instructed, and then I tried to explain it to him. "That bright star is Mercury, and it moves because the earth rotates. It does the same thing every night."

He looked at me funny. "Well, there are a lot of those lights moving and they can't be all stars."

Why couldn't he understand? Or was he a UFO believer? This amazed me, because his father was an educated man. Maybe this kid had never spent any time outside, under the stars before. In the end, I decided to let it go.

He had also brought a rifle along and told me how he was going to start an outfitting business hunting coyotes. He even slept with that rifle! I never carried a weapon any more than a knife in the outback, as what is there really to fear? There is more to fear walking down the streets of Chicago! I thought this kid had some serious growing up to do. How was he going to run an outfitting business if he was scared of the dark?

When I started working on getting the hole ready to excavate, he couldn't take the heat, so I gave him something to do under the shelter. When I was heading back to town to get some supplies at the end of the first week, he loaded up his gear and said he was leaving and wanted to be paid. To be honest, I didn't mind his decision as he hadn't been all that much help.

HEART MOUNTAIN

First stop was the bank and the second stop was his vehicle where I wished him all the best with his outfitting business.

I had been in contact with my father, and although he was now eighty-two, he wanted to be in on the adventure, so he flew down a week later. As my father was getting settled into our camp, the treasure hunting group arrived on site to see what I had accomplished and were excited to start digging. They had a cooler full of beer to celebrate the start of the venture. I prefer not to indulge when I am out in the desert, especially when I have explosives around. I decided to remind them why we were there and that it was dangerous work.

As they were all chatting away, telling tales of treasures, I thought it would be a good time to test some old explosive I got from a miner I knew to see if it was still good. I disappeared for a couple of minutes. I took one of the tubes of emulsion explosive and tied a blasting cap and a two-foot-long black powder fuse cord to it. I lit the fuse cord and threw the explosive in the dry creek bed underneath an overhanging tree. I went back inside the shelter and stood there as they were busy talking and drinking. When the explosive went off, they almost jumped out of their skins. I told them I was just testing the explosives, but in reality I did it to get their attention and to let them know that I meant business while we were out there. I will say from then on that I got paid promptly every week!

The next day, we moved our winch, explosives, and drills up to the site of the shaft and started sinking a four-by-five-foot hole going down. I had brought my father's ATV with us on the back of my truck, and I cleared a path up the side of the mountain for him to ride it to where we were going to work. After going down six feet, I connected a fan blowing unit to a small generator we had brought. A four-inch PVC pipe was fastened to one corner of the shaft and hooked to the fan to supply fresh air down in the hole. This kept me cool while I worked in the shaft, and we also used the fan unit for flushing out the dust and fumes after a blast.

    Prior to this I had rented an air compressor, which weighed 1,500 pounds. Mounted on skids, we loaded it onto the bed of my one-ton truck and unloaded it at the site. The mountainous terrain was too rough to tow an air compressor behind my truck. I then piped compressed air 400 feet up the side of the mountain thorough a one-inch PVC pipe so we could use an air drill for drilling holes in the rock for explosives. My father would be at the top of the shaft with the winch and lower the thirty-gallon bucket he made so that I could fill it with loose material. Once filled, he would hoist it out and dump it over to the side. Once I hit solid material again, he would drop down the air drill so that I could drill one-and-a-half-inch holes down three feet. This was the tough part—the dust from the drill was so thick you couldn't see more than six inches in front of you. I wore safety goggles and had a towel wrapped around my face and neck so that I wouldn't breathe the dust. At the end of the day my shirt would be stiff from the sweat and dust. I would always start off with a clean shirt, but it didn't stay clean long. I would beat out my pants over a rock to get rid of the dust so that I could get a couple of days of use out of a pair.

    Once the holes were drilled, my father would pull out the air drill and send down the explosives so that I could charge each hole with twelve inches of explosive with a piece of detonation cord attached and sticking up out of the blast hole. Then I would add twenty-four inches of packing or stemming as it is called, generally small gravel, which helps stop the explosive gases from escaping thus creating a better blast and fragmentation. I then attached a three-foot fuse to a blasting cap that was connected with detonation cord to all the blast holes. The three-foot fuse, once lit, gave me three minutes to climb out of the hole before the explosives went off. I thought that was plenty of time, but my father always gave me a rash of shit for cutting the fuse cord so short. I told him I was trying to be economical! Once the explosives went off, I had to get back down into the hole and do a quick check to make sure all the explosives had gone off before I started digging again.

It was simple, but back breaking and dangerous work. Drilling, hammering, and shoveling took a toll on my joints. At night, my joints would start aching and by early morning I couldn't sleep anymore. I always stocked up on Tiger Balm to rub my muscles and joints to help relieve the pain so that I could get a little sleep. But this was part of the gig! I wasn't thinking about the toll it was taking on my body and how it would affect my joints in twenty or thirty years.

Once every ten days we would go to Apache Junction for an overnight stay at a motel to do our laundry, get more supplies, and fill our five-gallon water jugs. We looked forward to the nice clean sheets, warm shower, and air-conditioned room at the motel, and the next morning's breakfast of biscuits and gravy. It was good to get away from being down in that hole every day. It seemed like the earth would just suck all my energy out.

When we got back to camp, I made sure we checked our cots and bedding before going to bed the next night. One time I found a scorpion under my dad's pillow. Scorpions are under just about every rock or chunk of wood out in the desert, so one had to be careful—their sting can be painful. One night, while we were sitting in our shelter with the lantern on, a large tarantula came wandering across the floor. I quickly took a broom and pushed it back outside. A couple of days later I saw a large tarantula wasp going into a hole and killing a tarantula before laying its eggs on the body. Nature is amazing to watch! I just didn't want any of that happening in our shelter.

The nights were magical out in the desert. We were far enough out of Phoenix that the lights from the city didn't interfere with the way you saw the universe and the millions of stars. We could hear a female mountain lion as she cried out in answer to her little ones. Listening closely, you could hear her and her cubs as she carried them around the top edge of the mountain above us. The javelinas would also come around at night and you could hear them rooting the ground and foraging for food. I didn't mind them as they generally kept snakes away.

In four weeks, we reached the forty-foot level with the sides cribbed and a ladder going all the way down to the bottom. However, we still couldn't see any indication of a tunnel or treasure room that was supposed to be down there. I told the group that the best thing to do was to get in touch with a geophysicist I knew who could perform a sounding on the sides of the shaft. Using a side-scan radar, he could detect any anomalies, empty "rooms," or dense objects. They agreed to hire him. We weren't there the day he did the sounding, but when I came back, they told me that the geophysicist had picked up a small anomaly, which couldn't be it, so we needed to go another forty feet. I told them the price just went up to $350 per foot.

The hole was getting deeper and taking longer to dig, but the treasure hunting group didn't want to give up. After the sounding, I would have cut my losses, but people chasing the dream of gold don't want to face failure. The promoters made the money guy believe that we were close, so he kept throwing his money at it. One of the promoters even had some prayer beads, and I heard him meditating and praying to Sathya Sai Baba, a holy man from India, to help the treasure materialize. I thought I might put in an order for some diamonds as well but didn't want to make him work too hard on all this materializing.

Finally, at eighty feet, I hit a white caliche-type material and told them that this was the end of the line. I wasn't going any further until they had another sounding done. I knew that what I was digging now was undisturbed material that had been there for a millennium. They weren't all that interested in another sounding, so I called it quits. I tore down my shelter and took everything that was mine but left the air compressor and the supply line as they said they would continue to pay rent on it. I told the owner of the compressor about the deal, and he agreed to keep renting it out to them, so I made sure an agreement was in place prior to my leaving.

After my father and I loaded up everything, I took him to the airport for a flight back to Denver. He had been a big help, and I don't know what I would have done without him. I paid him $60 per foot. First, he didn't want any of it but he earned every cent of it. He was still a tough old guy!

The group managed to find another fellow who went another thirty feet before they finally quit—at least that's what I heard. They ran out of money, and they couldn't pay the miner nor the guy they had leased the air compressor from. I made the right decision to leave; there wasn't anything there except an empty hole in the ground. Later on, I found out that they had never filed a mining claim, so they didn't have a permit to mine on the property. These promoters were out of touch with reality.

While digging the shaft I started looking around for possible Spanish markings in the area. The large rock that was next to the hole that I had dug had several arrows carved on the side of it and another rock had a "T" and "5" carved on it. This was in a remote area so not just anyone would have made these markings on the rocks. You couldn't really see them until the afternoon when the sun cast a shadow. What did it all mean? What was the real story about the markings on the rocks and designs on the mountain?

I was interested in the "special" camera that the guy claimed could see into the ground. I had researched all sorts of cameras and film and found out that Kodak made a special film that could determine different features on the ground, such as old trails and foundations. Infrared cameras were useful, but they could not pick up anything more than a foot or so underground. I made a call to the Jet Propulsion Laboratory in California and talked with a fellow there. The guy said that if there was such a camera, he wouldn't be sitting at his job; he would be out there looking for treasure with me. The camera thing was just another con that these so-called promoters—I mean, the money man—paid for!

I hiked around Heart Mountain and found a snake (or serpent) that was formed using rocks laid out in a long snake-like pattern. The head was a large rock that was in the form of a triangle. This pattern was lying on top of a ridge slightly to the east of Heart Mountain. In studying the Spanish signs in the books by Charles Kenworth, the serpent was supposed to point to where the treasure was. If you looked from the serpent's head across the dry wash, you could see a flat, vertical

HEART MOUNTAIN

rock with a Spanish marking on it, which referred to a mine shaft or a treasure. You could only see it in the afternoon as the sun cast a shadow, just as the Spanish map designers had meant for it to be seen.

The serpent and the carvings on the stone are possibly the real deal. I hope to go back with ground-penetrating radar to sound the stone with the markings on it. If this is the entrance to the treasure cave, then we will have our eureka moment.

CHAPTER FIFTEEN
Lost Confederate Gold

I was working out in Las Vegas for four years on and off while hunting for treasures from maps that John gave me. After leaving Las Vegas, I found work in Arizona and California but always made time between projects to go treasure hunting. Whenever I could, I would stop to see John in Strawberry and he would tell me stories. Even though John had to use a walker to get around at home, his mind was as sharp as ever. The following story was of a treasure that was supposed to be buried not far from where he lived, but he had searched for it with no luck.

He had a friend who was a writer at a treasure hunting magazine in the 1970s. The writer heard an interesting story from a Mexican fellow who lived around Flagstaff; he'd kept the story quiet for thirty-five years. The Mexican fellow told John's friend he would tell him the story, but the friend had to swear not to publish it.

The story goes that this fellow and a friend were deer hunting on the Mogollon Rim in 1935. They camped at a spring alongside the new Rim Road, and from there they went in a northerly direction into the rolling hills and woods to hunt. At about noon, one of the hunters shot a deer. It didn't go down, so they started tracking it by the blood spots it was leaving. When it was getting late and they still hadn't found the deer, they thought they had better head back to their camp before it got too dark. However, they had hiked a lot farther than they had thought and the sun was going down rapidly, so they decided to camp where they were and head back to their original camp in the morning.

They found a spot under an overhanging rock at the top of a small canyon. This overhanging rock was next to a long vertical rock face where they went to gather some old limbs for firewood. One of them noticed something that looked like the top of a nail keg buried in the ground. He cleaned off the top and opened it up. It was full of $20 gold pieces! Upon further digging, they found sixteen small nail kegs buried along the base of the outcrop. They took some of the $20 gold pieces and covered the kegs back up. Before heading back to camp the next morning, they noticed pieces of a wrecked wagon at the bottom of the ravine. All that was left was some wagon wheels and wood. They headed back to their camp, then decided to pack up and head back to town.

After they arrived back in town, they unpacked their gear and went to the liquor store to buy a bottle of whiskey to celebrate. They traded a $20 gold piece for the bottle of whiskey. At that time, it was illegal to own gold in the United States: a bill had been passed in 1933 limiting the ownership of gold, which wasn't repealed until Gerald Ford signed an order authorizing the ownership of gold in 1974. (This is a story in and of itself.)

When the bottle of whiskey was finished, they went home. The next morning, the Mexican telling the story went over to his friend's home. His wife said he was still sleeping in the bedroom and that he should go in and wake him up. He went

RANDOM TANGENTS

into the bedroom, but he wasn't sleeping—he was dead! After that, he considered the gold to be devil's gold, so he took the remaining coins and went to a place they called the "big hole" close to Flagstaff. He threw the coins in and never looked back. (I suspect this "big hole" could have been the meteorite crater just outside of Flagstaff.)

The Mexican hadn't told the story for thirty-five years, but as he was getting old, he thought it didn't matter anymore whether he told it or not. The one thing he wouldn't do was tell the location of the kegs, as he didn't want the curse to fall on someone else.

The treasure writer told all of this to John, and in time John went looking for it. He knew where the only spring was along the road, and he thought it would be easy to find the gold. But first he wanted to verify the story. He found out that the story went all the way back to the Civil War, when Confederate Army soldiers had buried a lot of gold coins in kegs along a railway before being taken prisoners by the Union. Two of these soldiers later refused to swear allegiance to the Union and escaped. They confiscated a sturdy wagon with a strong team of horses and went to dig up the gold. They loaded sixteen of the kegs onto the wagon and headed west toward California to meet up with some Confederate sympathizers.

As they traveled, they met a small wagon train going to California and asked if they could join them. As they were nearing Indian country in Arizona, they thought it better to be in a group for protection. For the night, they all rested at a stage stop before getting to Chavez Pass. The man that worked at the stage stop later said that one of the wagons seemed heavily loaded. He said that the two men on the wagon had southern accents and their wagon was the last one in the wagon train. That was the last he saw any of the wagons.

Near Chavez Pass, they were attacked by Indians and they quickly circled their wagons so they could have a better chance of protecting themselves. All the wagons circled except for the one driven by the two men with the southern accents. Instead, they took off as fast as they could to get away, and it looked like they might have made it. But why didn't the Indians chase them? John said that the Indians knew the country and they could catch up to them later, so they focused on the wagon train first.

In the end, the small wagon train succumbed to the attacks and there were no survivors. A short time later an Army patrol found the wagon train and buried the dead. They also found wagon tracks heading south, which they followed until it started raining and the tracks disappeared. No one ever saw the wagon again! John's theory was that the soldiers drove the wagon up Long's Valley into the canyon, carried the gold kegs up the slope, and buried them against the rock face.

I memorized everything he said and headed to Las Vegas to start a job to make some money. During that spring and summer, I saved up some money and called my father to see if he and my son would want to go on a treasure hunt in August. They were both in, so we set up a plan. I was to come back to Denver and drive my father's van and trailer with the ATV to Arizona. My son was still out of school, so we had time to camp out for a couple of weeks and enjoy the cool high country on the Mogollon Rim.

When I arrived in Denver, I went to the Denver Federal Center and picked up some topographical maps of the area so we would have a better understanding of the terrain. We

RANDOM TANGENTS

loaded up my father's van and headed south. When we got to Winslow, Arizona, we turned south on Highway 87 for fifty miles until we got to a gas station and restaurant at Clints Well. We fueled up and checked out the restaurant before heading down the road and turning back into the national forest on the Rim Road, now labeled Forest Road 300. We spent the week camping and hiking up and down Long's Canyon searching for clues.

My son and I walked both sides of that canyon around every rock or outcrop that looked like anything that would match the description in search of the treasure. We had two types of metal detectors: a standard loop detector and my two-box metal detector, which was supposed to find large objects and voids in the ground. We looked up any side ravines that could possibly fit the story, but we couldn't find anything that resembled pieces of an old wagon. The weather was usually nice early in the morning and by late afternoon rain and lightning storms seemed to start coming in, so we made sure we were back to camp by then.

On the first Sunday, we headed over to the little restaurant and gas station because they had a Sunday special on blueberry pancakes. My son and father both loved them; they were the size of a plate and full of plump blueberries, so that was our treat for the week. Both my son and my father were getting tired of my cooking.

The following week, my son and I took off in another direction and found a small swimming hole and took advantage of it. On our way back to the camp, we got caught in one heck of a storm. We found a place under a large rock next to a stream to shelter us. As it continued to pour, I started to worry about the stream, knowing that we had to cross it to get back to camp.

LOST CONFEDERATE GOLD

We decided we weren't going to get that much wetter, and the lightning had let up, so we took off and made it back to the van. My father opened the van door laughing at the two drowned rats standing there. After we got dry clothes on and warmed up, the sun came out and it turned into another beautiful day.

When we got back to Denver, I headed back to Las Vegas again as there was a lot of work out there at the time. On long weekends, I would head back over to the Mogollon Rim and camp out overnight as I searched some other areas. Finally, I decided that maybe John was wrong in his assumption about which canyon the Mexican hunters had ended up in. I started searching into canyons east of Kehl Spring.

At that time, I occasionally stopped in Sedona to see my friends Larry and Karen. She told me about using horary astrology to find things and explained how it worked. She said that if you asked a question at a certain time, the position of the stars could give you the answer you were looking for. She had a friend named Tom down in Florida who was the best horary astrologer she knew, and she offered to put me in contact with him. She said that Tom had even been asked to go to Egypt to locate ruins and tombs. This was promising! I thought I would give it a try as I had nothing to lose and everything to gain.

Since I had written off Long's Canyon, I studied my topographical maps to see which other canyon could fit the story. Soon after talking to Karen, I went back to the area with a plan. I went down the canyon I had chosen as most probable. When I reached the dry stream bed at the bottom, I laid some branches on the ground in the form of a cross. I then went back up to the pay phone at the small gas station and called Tom.

I asked him, "In what direction and what distance does the treasure I seek lie from where I have laid the crossed branches

RANDOM TANGENTS

in the stream bed?" Tom said to call back the next day. I called him the next day, and he gave me a direction and an approximate distance. I went back out to where I laid the branches and proceeded as he had directed. Reaching the approximate distance, I placed another marker—this time with three stacked stones. Again, I went back to the gas station and made the call to Tom and asked the same question but used the three stones as the starting location. I did this a total of three times and by the third time, I knew that the treasure had to be within the triangle that were formed with the markers. I had carefully marked the three spots on my topographical map so I would know the area I would need to search.

It wasn't a large triangle, and I could cover most of it in a day, but it was up and down small canyons, so it took a bit of searching. On the second day I found an overhanging rock and underneath looked to be charcoal remains of an old campfire. Also, there was a rock outcrop next to the overhanging rock that was a sheer face for twenty feet or so. I searched at the base of this rock outcropping with my metal detector but couldn't find anything. Was I in the right place?

I decided to camp out that night on the other side of the ravine. I found a dirt road that saved me a lot of hiking from where I had parked earlier in the day. I sat up camp about one hundred yards down this dirt road from the main road. At the turnoff from the main road were some large rocks I had noticed that looked out of place. I got a funny feeling there, but I couldn't make out why. That night when I tried to sleep, I noticed there was not a single sound around me. It was deathly quiet. I didn't sleep well and left the next day still thinking about it.

LOST CONFEDERATE GOLD

I decided to take a trip down to Goldfield, just north of Apache Junction and talk to a fellow I knew there. Dave knew how to use dowsing rods, or "witching sticks," to find things. Most people have heard of using dowsing rods, clothes hangers, or a willow branch to find water but Dave had learned how to use them to find other things of value. He made his own dowsing rods, and whatever he was looking for, he would put a piece of that material on the end of his rods. Dave had found a million-dollar gold vein that he mined and also a stagecoach chest from a robbery. I asked him if he would go up on the Mogollon Rim with me to see if he could get a pull on the treasure that I was looking for. I know that many people consider dowsing a farce, and to be honest, I came across a lot of dowsers who couldn't find their way out of a paper bag. However, I trusted Dave's skills.

We drove up to the Rim, and I took him to where I had camped out to see what he might pick up on. He got out his dowsing rods with a piece of gold on the end and slowly started turning in a circle to get a feel of the area. When he stopped, his dowsing rods were pointing slightly downward from the top of the ridge across from us. He said he had a pull over there. I hadn't told him anything, but he was pointing right to the rock face where the gold should have been buried. But what if the treasure was no longer there? I had read that things (as well as people) leave psychic imprints even after they are gone, even though this has not been proven scientifically.

As it started to rain, I thought it best to get back to a solid road to make sure we were able to get out. I told him that maybe we could come back later and find a way over to the other side as he was an older fellow who had difficulty hiking up and down rough terrain.

RANDOM TANGENTS

My brother, Jim, had started working with me in Las Vegas, and one weekend I took him over to the same area just to look it over. We drove to the exact same spot where I had camped out and where I had taken my friend Dave the dowser. As we were walking towards the big rocks at the turn in the road, he said he got a funny feeling. As we got closer, he stopped abruptly and turned around with the hair standing up on his arms and tears rolling down his face.

"Jim, what is wrong?"

"I can't go any closer to those large rocks. Indian women and children were massacred there. I can feel it. It is a very sad place."

"I also experienced a feeling of death when I camped out here. There was nothing alive around here."

"Let's go back to the car. I need to get away from this spot."

I knew there was a strange energy there, and he was more sensitive than I was; I believed him. After hiking around for a while, we headed back to Las Vegas.

Later, I did a little research of the area, especially Battleground Ridge, which runs north from the old Crook Trail on the top of the Mogollon Rim. It was named after the Battle of Big Dry Wash, which was the last battle in Arizona between the Apache and the U.S. Army on July 17, 1882. According to different accounts, there were around twenty Apache Indians and one soldier killed. The dead Apache Indians were left where they fell, and the soldier was buried with a marker on his grave. As military history was poorly documented at the time, I wouldn't be surprised if a massacre had occurred in the area.

Winter was coming to the high country, so I didn't have much time to go back. I went one last weekend so I could spend the night up there just to have one final look. When I

LOST CONFEDERATE GOLD

woke up in the morning in my little pup tent, I looked out and big snowflakes were falling everywhere. I knew I had to get out of there as I was five miles off the main road. As I hurriedly stepped out of my tent, a whole herd of elk ran by me. They knew I meant them no harm; I had seen many up on the rim before. It was freedom and nature at its best! I finally made it out even though I had to move a fallen tree off the road as the snow was accumulating quickly.

The next spring, when the snow had melted on the Mogollon Rim, I decided to take one last stab at this treasure. My plan was to take Karen, my astrologer friend, with me to see if she could tell me anything. I took her to the overhanging rock and told her the story. She touched the rock and closed her eyes for a minute and told me what she saw: The soldiers didn't drive the wagon in from the bottom but took the high road to get here. They buried the kegs of gold coins along the rock ledge, disconnected the wagon from the horses, and then shoved the wagon over the edge, which then landed in the bottom of the ravine. She said the soldiers got on the horses and were going to ride out of there, but they didn't get far before the Indians caught up to them.

The two Mexicans found the kegs of coins in 1935 but left them there. So, who found them between that time and now? Did the story get out to someone else and they beat me to it? Did loggers working in the area stumble upon them? Was I close but just didn't find them? Who knows! I felt I had given this treasure hunt my best attempt and could walk away from it knowing that the kegs probably weren't there anymore. I never looked back!

One of the last times I visited John in Strawberry, he went into his closet and brought out an old cardboard box full of his treasure maps. He had already told me the stories for most of them and proceeded to tell me the remaining stories. After that, he wanted to give me the box of maps saying that nobody wanted to hear his stories anymore. I handed the box back to him and told him to hang on to it as I would be back again to see him. What else did he have to live for other than talking about his years of treasure hunting?

I researched and looked for each one of the treasures connected to the maps over a period of nine years from 1994 until 2003. When I first started treasure hunting it was all about finding the treasure and the excitement. As time went along my whole attitude changed; I used treasure hunting as an excuse to disappear and be alone with my thoughts. It was a way to disconnect from the daily world of chatter and rush. I was becoming more aware of nature, the universe, and searching for meaning. Sleeping under the stars with the sounds of the night led me into a deeper spiritual journey.

Around this time, I was studying different eastern philosophies and came across two questions that I wanted to find the answers for. Who am I? And why am I here? I know it will be a lifelong quest to find the answers, but how long is life anyway?

CHAPTER SIXTEEN
Lost Meteorite

The following story started out when John told me about a good friend of his, a fellow named Mitchell. It seems Mitchell was working in Parker, Arizona, in 1920 or so for the railroad when a meteorite went over the town. It was so low that the energy wave created by it turned over empty fifty–five-gallon barrels! Mitchell decided to go looking for it and set off with his horse and pack burro. At first, he thought that it had possibly hit a mountain some miles away; that was his first destination. When he arrived, he met up with a small clan of Indians who told him that they had seen it, but it had continued toward the Chuckwalla Mountains. As he got closer to those mountains, he ran into an old prospector who had also seen the meteorite and told Mitchell where it had landed.

The meteorite had been traveling at a tremendous velocity, so it cut a furrow in the ground for several hundred yards before coming to rest in a wash on the desert floor next to the mountains. Mitchell said that when he found the meteorite, it was buried about twenty feet deep and from what he could see, it was about nine feet across on the top. He found a small piece about the size of a five-pound flour sack lying next to it, and when he tried to pick it up, it felt like a lead weight.

Mitchell took a sample and sent it to San Francisco to have it assayed to see if there were any precious minerals in it. It was a heavy nickel-iron meteorite, of which only about 10 percent enter our atmosphere. The rest mostly disintegrate and if anything is left, it is basically a cinder. According to the assay, there was platinum in the meteorite valued at $12 per pound. It sounded good, but back in the 1920s, he didn't have the mining equipment or the financing to break apart this meteorite to recover it for the minerals.

Mitchell told the story to John and their friend, Page, while setting around a campfire one night. A few years later, John received a sixteen-page letter from Page detailing how he went looking for the meteorite. He had driven out on the old sandy road getting stuck several times before coming to a small brown rock hill he thought to be the proper location. He took out a dip needle (which is like a compass turned on its side and draws toward metal objects) to see if he could find the meteorite. He started walking around and came across a spot alongside a shallow wash that drew his needle down. Page believed this to be the spot and marked it by making two stacked stone markers one of which was about thirty feet back from the wash so it wouldn't be lost in a flash flood.

In the 1950s, John finally went looking for the meteorite himself. He said that when he was looking for the turnoff road from the highway, he stopped and talked to a lady at a small ranch. She told him that a few years earlier her husband went out back to chase down the chickens and picked up a handful of rocks to throw at them. He found what looked like metal pieces in the rock. Curiosity got to him, so he mailed the metal pieces in for an assay. It turned out that it was high-grade platinum ore. John figured that what the rancher found must have been drippings off the meteorite. He was on the right trail!

LOST METEORITE

John found the road and went on back alongside the mountain according to the directions Mitchell had given him. On reaching the area, which had a large brown outcrop sticking up and setting out from the main mountain, John started walking down to an old wash where he believed the meteorite to be. Even though there was no trace of it, he was sure he was at the right place, so he filled out a blank mining claim form to file a claim on the area. After filling it out, he placed it in a Prince Albert tobacco tin. These tins were used a lot for this purpose as one could stuff the claim paper in them and tie them upside down on a wooded stake or leave them in a pile of rock and they would keep your claim paper dry. After tying the tin to a wooden stake, John left the area figuring that one day he would come back and do some digging.

I did some due diligence on meteorites before setting off on this venture and found that no meteorite had been found to have platinum in it before, so this would indeed be rare if true. Even if it didn't have platinum in it, the price would still be astronomical. I read an article about the famous meteorite hunter, Robert Haag, aka the "meteorite man," who cut them and sold them for $10 to $20 per gram. I called and asked if he would be interested in buying a large meteorite if I happened to find it, and he told me to call him when I located it.

While in Denver, I found a geophysicist who helped me build a computer model to determine what size of an anomaly I would be getting on a proton magnetometer based on the size, depth, and composition of the meteorite. A proton magnetometer is used to measure the gravitational field of the earth. When walking over a large metal object, it will register a change in the magnetic field in that area creating the anomaly.

RANDOM TANGENTS

I asked my father if he wanted to go on another trip. He was always happy to get away as my mother was involved with her bookstore six days a week. We loaded up his van and hooked up the trailer with the ATV on it. Before leaving, we went down to the local Army surplus store for some gloves and things. I saw a large white parachute that I could use for a shade out in the desert, so I purchased it too. I was hoping that by draping it over the van, I could create a large shady area. It was September but still hot in the desert.

When we arrived at Desert Center, we went south down Summit Road and took a left on Red Cloud Mine Road until we came to a good camping area, which at least had some brush and a little cover around it. From here we could go up and search the canyon for the meteorite. Just a little distance from camp also was Gas Line Road where we could turn right and go down until we came to the area that Page had described.

After getting situated, I would head out early in the morning while it was still cool and take a one-gallon jug of water. In the first few days, I found John's claim marker he had left forty years prior. The claim paper inside the old Prince Albert tobacco tin was getting a little brittle and crisp after sitting out in the desert all these years, but I could still read his name.

The proton magnetometer was mounted onto my backpack and I attached the small display showing the gravitational field to my belt. I must have walked every square foot within a half mile of that claim marker and didn't see the anomaly I was looking for—not even close. I did see some smaller anomalies and thought they might be some tiny pieces, so I recorded readings on some of them.

One morning I went out early to dig in one of the areas where I had a small reading on my magnetometer. I had my metal detector with me and found a small piece of rock on the surface that was magnetic, so I held onto that for future examination. I dug down about five feet at this location but didn't find any indication of small meteorite pieces.

John had also heard that a group of county workers who were hauling gravel out of a canyon came across a meteorite and pushed it over to the side of the road. In looking at the topo map I suspect they had to be working up Red Cloud Mine Road. Father and I proceeded up Red Cloud Mine Road to where the old mine had been operating and looked around, but it was hopeless. We were looking for a needle in the haystack. After searching the canyon and the area where John thought the meteorite was, the next step was to try to find the stacked stones that Page had left, possibly marking another piece.

One morning I went down Gas Line Road, most probably the same road Page used, to an area that had several large mounds of dark brown rock. I had my proton magnetometer with me just checking the magnetic field while I searched the area. While walking around the mounds, I came across the two stacks of rocks that Page had left there. I was excited but not for long. As I paced out from the markers, I found a trench that was about thirty feet long and ended at a large, empty hole. My proton magnetometer didn't pick up any anomalies in this area, so it looked as though someone had beaten me to it. What I did notice in this area with the two large mounds of brown basalt rock was that the proton magnetometer was showing some fairly large fluctuations in the readings that were continually going up and down as though the earth had a heartbeat. I was curious and mapped the area of the magnetic field surrounding the two mounds. It was quite a large anomaly that was created just by these two mounds.

RANDOM TANGENTS

While there, a funny thing happened. The whole area was next to the Chocolate Mountain Aerial Gunnery Range. At that time, it wasn't unusual to see jets flying low through the mountains, as the Navy Top Gun pilots from Miramar, California, were training through here. One day after I came back from searching my father said that a military jeep had approached our camp. I think that the jets flying over that day had reported seeing the white parachute on the ground, and they came out to see if a pilot had gone down. When they saw our white canopy parachute, they laughed, turned around, and left.

The desert has a unique ecosystem. One morning, I noticed over thirty desert tortoises crawling on the desert floor toward the mountain. I realized later that I had witnessed the migration of an endangered species! A couple of days later I found one up on the mountain when I went hiking one morning. I was amazed that he had crawled up that high from the desert floor.

One time while out by myself, I was sitting on the rear tailgate of my truck eating a can of beans. When I finished, I was going to put the empty can in my trash bag but thought I would throw it down on the ground for a while to see if there were any ants or small animals that wanted to clean up the inside. In a short time, I caught movement out of my left eye. It was a small desert fox. What a kick! The smell of the beans must have traveled a long way.

One caution if you go hiking early in the morning on a foot or animal path: Watch out for rattlesnakes. The material of the paths has been compressed over time and holds heat better overnight, so the rattlesnakes lie on the paths to keep warm. Rattlesnakes are usually pretty sluggish early in the morning

LOST METEORITE

on a cool day. As the sun comes up and the heat increases, they slither back under cover to get out of the sun. Beware!

Another time I was out there in the spring after it had rained and was enjoying the ocotillo and other desert plants that were blooming. As I was walking across the desert floor I crossed paths with a badger and was quite surprised. It went on its way and I went on mine. I found some underground water tanks that had been placed close to the mountains, probably by a government or environmental agency, to help the small animals and bird life in that area. I had been wondering where the birds were getting their water from and thought there had to be a spring in the area until I found these underground tanks. If you see birds and small animals around, there must be water.

Father and I stayed out there for a little over three weeks and went to Indio a couple of times to stock up on food. Once we had to get the van heater box washed out. A desert rat had got into our van and worked its way into the fan cage of the heater. Once there, it couldn't get out and died. In a couple of days, it began to smell, and I had to dig around to find out where the smell was coming from. This happened again, but as soon as I smelled it the second time, we took off to town to clean it out again. One hell of a good rat trap!

While going to Indio from Desert Center, we stopped at the General George Patton Memorial Museum in Chiriaco Summit. The museum was informative about the area and how General Patton trained over one million men there to fight in conditions similar to the Sahara Desert of northern Africa during World War II. There is a lot of history in this area even though it seems so desolate.

During the time we were there, the temperatures were getting up to 115 degrees, so we were ready to call it quits. When we arrived in Denver, I headed to the Federal Center, which had experienced geologists on staff. I gave them the small piece of magnetic rock I had picked up and asked if it was a piece of meteorite. They said they would have to take a thin slice and examine it. A week later, the geologists let me know that the rock that I had found was a piece of magnetite and not a meteorite. Close, but no cigar! But why didn't I find the big piece that John thought was in the wash?

While in the Federal Center, I found a fellow who had extensive experience with proton magnetometers. I went to his office, introduced myself, and explained what I had been doing. I handed him the pages of recorded data that I had compiled on small anomalies that I thought could be something. He looked at the data and just laughed! He said that what I had recorded was the result of lightning. He told me that when lightning strikes the desert sand, it creates a magnetic anomaly—that is what I had picked up on with the proton magnetometer. I learned something!

At the Federal Center, I ordered an aerial photo of the area that had been taken years before and had it blown up as big as they could, which was about three-by-three feet. When the photo arrived, it was good enough to be able to pick out cacti or trees in the area. I took it with me and stopped in Congress, Arizona, to see a fellow who had done some map dowsing for me before on the gold adventure in Mexico. Since he seemed accurate, I thought I would let him try and see if he could find the meteorite on the large photograph. He started dowsing and finally made one mark on the photo. He said that was the only place on the photo that he had a draw to. I thought that the next time down there, I would see if there was anything at the spot he marked.

LOST METEORITE

When I had the chance to return to the area later, I started walking and identifying the cacti and trees in the photo. I was able to walk right to the spot the dowser had marked on the photo and sticking out of the ground was a piece of a six-inch iron pipe. That was it! He had found iron but not what I was looking for.

Prior to starting this venture, I had purchased a topographical map of the area and still had it when I stopped by to visit my mother at her bookstore in Englewood, Colorado. She said she knew a Mexican lady that came into her bookstore who was sort of a physic and read crystal balls and maybe she could help me locate the meteorite. As I said before, I would try anything, so why not? I brought the topographical map to the bookstore and met this lady. I gave her the map and she told me to give her a week or so.

I waited two weeks and gave her a call, and she said she was done reading the map. She described everything she had seen with her crystal ball on the map. She said that she had seen an eagle flying down from the top left corner of the map and then she went on to describe a fellow dressed in what seemed to be World War I Army gear, who was out in this area with a horse looking for something. I knew that she had just described John's friend, Mitchell, and the eagle to the upper left-hand corner would be Eagle Mountain, which wasn't on this map. She also told me that she believed that some men had taken the meteorite out in pieces in 1929. It was the end of another hunt, but at least I learned a lot more about the magnetic fields of the earth, the history of the area, and the survival of animals in the desert. You always gain something from each adventure in life. Another thing that I read was that the Native Americans slept with their heads pointed north as they would align with the magnetic poles of the earth and sleep better. Eastern philosophy also States that the body is magnetically charged. It all makes sense when you think about it. Since that time, I always try to make it a priority to sleep with my head to the north so that I have a better night's sleep. It may sound a little crazy but try it yourself for a while and see if it works.

CHAPTER SEVENTEEN
Treasure on the Colorado

This story takes us to an area on the Colorado River about thirty miles north of Yuma, Arizona, as the crow flies. It was about 1850 and four gunmen had just robbed the Army payroll wagon of $30,000 in gold coin and were fleeing the crime scene. When they came to the Colorado River it was too much to carry across the river, so they buried the gold next to a mesquite tree on the California side. They quickly searched for a place to cross the river and found a crossing spot just after the river made a big northerly bend towards Arizona. They swam their horses across and started working their way south along the riverbank. In a short time, the cliffs of the mountain were right along the river's edge, not leaving a lot of room for travel. They noticed a cave and decided to camp there for the night.

One of the outlaws went down to the sand bar in the river and dug a hole in it so that the river water would filter through the sand, thereby providing clear drinking water. As the outlaw was digging, he noticed something that looked like gold nuggets in the sand and every scoop had some in it. He summoned the others, who confirmed that these were indeed gold nuggets.

RANDOM TANGENTS

They knew the nuggets had to come from a vein somewhere. They looked up the mountain and saw a six-inch-wide quartz vein in the cliff above, so they worked their way up to it and started chiseling it with whatever tools they had. They saw that there was more gold in the vein, so they decided to go back to California to get more tools and provisions.

In a couple of days, they brought back everything they needed, including four Mexican laborers to help them. As they continued to work the vein, they amassed a large cache of gold nuggets. During this time, they made friends with a band of Indians who were camped at Yuma Wash, just a couple of miles away. They paid the Indians to take care of their horses while they were working the vein.

One day, a fight broke out between one of the outlaws and an Indian brave, which ended in the shooting of the Indian. Now the outlaws were worried that the Indians would go to the Army fort and report the incident. They took their horses, loaded the gold nuggets, and led them up the ridge above the river to a flat area. There they had the Mexicans dig a four-foot-deep hole where they would bury the nuggets. They had to make two trips with their horses to get all the nuggets up to the place where they buried them. They covered the hole and made sure there wasn't any evidence of their digging, then set up a couple of marker rocks some distance from the hole.

After covering the hole, they took the four Mexicans down to the river and shot them, making sure they were dead before they left. That night as three of the outlaws sat around a campfire and the fourth was on his horse, a posse looking for cattle rustlers came riding in and a gunfight broke out that killed the three outlaws around the campfire and wounded the fourth as he was riding away.

TREASURE ON THE COLORADO

The fourth outlaw made it back to Missouri where his sister and her husband ran a grocery store. He stayed there until the bullet wound in his hip healed. He eventually told the story of finding and burying the nuggets to his sister's family and produced a couple that he was carrying in his pocket. His sister's husband and son wanted to go right then and dig up the nuggets, but the outlaw told them it was too dangerous as the Indians were on the warpath in the west at that time.

As the years went by, the husband and the outlaw brother died, leaving the woman with a failing grocery store. Her son decided to go and find the stash of gold nuggets. He traveled west to Yuma and found a local rancher who outfitted him with horses and supplies. After thirty days, the boy gave up and left, never to be seen again.

During the search the rancher saw the map the boy had, and later told John's father about it. On the map it showed a pointer rock in the river, a cave, and a pile of rocks up on a ridge that were placed to show where the nuggets were buried. But when the boy got to where the marker rocks should have been, he noticed that a sign had been erected alongside the river by using the stones in the area. The boy believed that the stones he was looking for had also been used for the sign, so he had no way of telling exactly where the nugget cache was.

Since the time of the outlaws in the 1850s, there has been a lot of activity in the area. In the early 1860s mines were opened for silver, lead, copper, and gold close to the river. The mines fluctuated in production and finally closed entirely in the late 1970s. There were several mines along the Arizona side of the river with steamboats running up and down the river from the Gulf of California to Castle Dome, Eureka and Norton's Landings carrying ore, supplies, mail, and passengers.

RANDOM TANGENTS

Also, since the time of the story, two dams have been built on the river, which means that the river is probably sixty to eighty feet above its original riverbed at places. The forty-three-feet-high Laguna Dam was built in 1909 for irrigation. Then, in 1938 they completed the Imperial Dam upstream of the Laguna Dam at a height of eighty-five feet. The Imperial Dam backed up 160,000 acre-feet of water, which covered 5,700+ acres, and since its construction, the area has mostly silted in. This story takes place along the stretch of river upstream of the Imperial Dam.

In the 1950s, John studied the area and flew up and down the river several times looking at the bends and matching the story to the terrain. He found an old miner living on the California side of the river who had known the area prior to the construction of the dams. The old miner told John where the pointer rock was and where he thought the cave might have been along the river.

With this information, John determined that the ridge jutting out the farthest into the river downstream from the pointer rock and the big bend in the river had to be the spot where the gold was buried. He and a couple of his friends spent several weeks digging and moving tons of material by hand in search for the gold nuggets, but in the end, they had to give up. John told me that he had used an old naval metal detector but couldn't find anything with it. I wasn't surprised—those old navy metal detectors only detected iron and wouldn't have picked up non-ferrous metals such as gold or silver!

I started my search for the nugget treasure by obtaining the topographical maps to the area and then going to the Western history section of the Denver Public Library to research old maps showing the Colorado River as well as pictures taken prior to the building of the dams. I also researched how much the river would have risen once the dams were built. I compared the old maps to the current topographical maps to see if the area in John's story was under water now. The pointer rock he told me about was under water, so it was of no help as to an exact location. As the river had risen, one probably wasn't going to find the quartz vein with the gold in it because it is now under water. Also, the vein might have been mined out after the outlaws left the area and before the dams were built. John also said that the nuggets were buried on a saddle or low area between two peaks. This low area would also have been easier digging due to loose material accumulating there over the years from the higher peaks.

The last piece of information that John shared with me was that the $30,000 in gold coins had been found by a rancher when he was clearing out an area that had an old dead mesquite tree and buried alongside it was the gold. This made me think that the story had some validity to it.

After doing all the research, I thought it was time to go down to Yuma and head up the Colorado River to Martinez Landing, which seemed to be the best place to start the search since it lay some distance downstream from the big turn in the river. After studying the old and the current maps, I was confident as to where John had thought the nuggets were buried. Not far upstream from Martinez Landing is Yuma Wash, which is where the Indians had been camped out so between there and the big bend in the river there had to be a ridge that the nuggets were buried on.

I found a four-wheel drive road along the edge of the river after leaving Martinez Lake that got me to Yuma Wash. From there I hiked along the edge of the river working my way back and forth to avoid the water and sloughs that are now prime duck hunting areas. After hiking for four hours, I came across an old miner's cabin which was close to the old Eureka Mine. I was still quite a distance from Norton's Landing and decided to call it a day and head back. As I was driving back to Martinez Lake, a five-foot rattlesnake crossed the sand road and I ran over him. When I looked in my rear-view mirror, it seemed pissed. I don't think I hurt him that much as the truck tires had buried him in the sand, but I wasn't going to get out to see if it was alright! He would have made a nice belt though!

The next day I rented a boat at Martinez Landing and went up to where the big bend was in the river and close to the old Norton's Landing. A large rock outcropping jutted out into the river and it was easy to tell that this was the area John and his friends thought the treasure was buried. It had a lot of holes and diggings on it. John was right; this looked like the most likely location considering the story. I boated back down the river to Martinez Landing looking for locations that could match the story.

I spent my first trip there just looking over the area to get a feel for it and to see what I needed when I came back to look further. Later that fall I asked my father if he was interested in taking off for a couple of weeks to do some fishing and look for some gold nuggets. We drove from Denver in his camper van and camped out for a few days around Martinez Lake. We rented a small boat and went up the river to have a have a look. We went past the big bend in the river just enjoying the ride. I found out quickly that you had to watch out for the sand bars and shallow areas in the river or else you would be out pushing yourself off one. My father wasn't impressed with my navigation skills after I had to get out and push us off a couple of times.

The next day I went back up the river to the place where John thought the nuggets were. I left my father at Martinez Landing with his fishing pole as he wanted to fish. I took my two-box, deep-penetrating metal detector with me. Even though I had thought it shouldn't be a problem to locate that large cache of nuggets down four feet, after searching and sounding the area, I had no luck. So where were the nuggets? Were they under water or was I at the wrong location?

I finally got back to Martinez Landing late in the afternoon and my father was still fishing. He had nine catfish on his stringer. I was impressed! I started skinning them as my uncle had taught me, but they had a barb on their back by their dorsal fin, and it hurt when you got stuck by it. I decided to fillet them and managed to get the job done quickly and without pain. (I had learned to fillet fish in Australia.) My father loves tartar sauce on his fish, so he went to the little grocery store nearby and bought some. After dinner I noticed that the tartar sauce had an odd greenish color to it. It had probably been sitting on a shelf in the store all summer! My father got sick and he blamed it on the catfish. Sometimes it's better not to argue.

I don't give up easily so I needed another plan to decide where the gold nugget stash could be. I contacted my friend Dave and asked if he wanted to try his hand at dowsing a cache of nuggets along the Colorado River. He said he would go along with me and see what we might be able to find, so I made arrangements to meet up with him in Yuma.

I rented a small boat again at Martinez Landing and we headed up the river. He had taped some gold nuggets on the end of his dowsing rods so he could get a pull. He started moving them back and forth at the ridges as we got close. He said that he didn't get any indication in the area John had searched. We continued up the river past the big bend and he did get a slight pull on some smaller ridges but nothing substantial.

In the end, nothing panned out on this treasure hunt, and after studying the maps again, I would say that there are several possibilities. One is that the spot is now under water, which I doubt. Another possibility is that the old rancher who took the nephew back to look for it went back later and found the stash. The last possibility would be that John was mistaken about the location. Maybe the stash was located close to one of the other bends in the river that are not as pronounced. The river looked much different in 1850 from today. I believe the gold is still out there, but I spent enough time on it. No looking back!

In this area there were many things to discover and learn: the history of the dams that were built and how water was controlled for irrigation, the history of the mining towns along the river and what they produced, and the history of the riverboats that once were prevalent here while the Colorado River ran free.

Today the area that was the possible place for the buried gold nuggets on the Arizona side of the Colorado River is now all part of the Imperial Wildlife Refuge. Across the river on the California side is the Picacho State Recreation Area which has camping and boat ramps. Downstream at the Imperial Dam Recreation Area there is long term camping offered along with boat ramps. The Colorado River in these areas during the summer is in full use with camping, boating and fishing up and down the river.

CHAPTER EIGHTEEN
The Lost Ivanpah Silver Vein

This is another treasure story that John had in his memory file that I believe had some merit to it. When John was a little boy, his family lived at a mining camp not far from Nipton, California. Today the mining camp is long gone and details of it probably don't exist as so many of these camps started and disappeared quickly. John's father, Ben, was a surveyor and miner at the turn of the century and traveled a lot.

Ben had a friend named McGill, who ran a small stage stop on Mesquite Lake, just to the north and west of Nipton, which was a dry lakebed. One day Ben stopped by to see McGill on his way to do some surveying for a mining company. As they sat talking, McGill asked him to survey a claim and file it for him. The claim would have Ben's name on it, because McGill wasn't a U.S. citizen, which meant he couldn't file the claim himself. In return, he wanted Ben to be an equal partner in the venture.

McGill had found a silver vein up the canyon from his stage station around a bend so you couldn't quite see it from there. He said he had pulled out some samples of the ore, which turned out to be high-grade silver. McGill was sure it could make them both rich once they started mining it. Ben was interested and said he would survey it as soon as he came back from the surveying job he was heading to. He returned in a few weeks to see how McGill was doing and to file the claim. When he arrived at the stage stop, McGill wasn't anywhere to be found. Concerned, Ben rode to the nearest town and asked about McGill. It turned out that McGill had taken sick and barely made it to town before he died.

As McGill had never shown the exact location of the vein to Ben and the claim was never filed. However, Ben told the story to his son, John, and the story was passed on to me. John further embellished the story with another story in the same area. He stated that there used to be another silver mine on the other side of the mountain. Allegedly, the silver vein in this Ivanpah Mine was so rich that they would blast it out and haul it directly to the smelter with very little processing. Allegedly, the vein was running 90 percent pure silver, and the mine had guards on every shipment to make sure they got to the smelter for refining.

One day when they set off another blast in the mine, they went in to start hauling out the silver ore and found that the vein had disappeared. The mountain had a fault line, or a sheer zone, that had interrupted the path of the vein. At that time, they didn't have any means to discern which way the vein continued so they had to shut down the mining operation. No silver, no mine! The mining company offered $100,000 to anyone who could find the continuation of the vein but there were no takers.

By telling me these two stories, John led me to believe that the silver vein that McGill had found was possibly on the same vein structure as the Ivanpah Mine. My focus on this adventure

THE LOST IVANPAH SILVER VEIN

would be looking for a high grade, possibly 90 percent pure silver vein. By studying the topographical map that John had given me, I could determine the area in which the old stage station was located. From there, it was easy to see which canyon McGill had been talking about.

John said he had been there several times looking but had never found anything. He said he was looking for a mine entrance or large excavation but never found any indication of either. I thought that if this vein was really 90 percent silver, it is going to be identifiable using an EM-31 instrument, which measures electromagnetic conductivity through the ground.

I rented an EM-31 and also took my two-box metal detector with me the first time I went out to the area. I had contacted my father and son, and they were in for a new adventure, so we loaded the van and ATV in Denver and headed out to Sandy Valley, about 45 miles south of Las Vegas.

When we got to Sandy Valley, there was a perimeter gravel road that ran all the way around the dry lakebed which was Mesquite Lake. At a crossroad that went across the lakebed and intersected the perimeter road was a corral and a windmill pumping water into a tank. We set up camp a couple of hundred yards in from the corral so we could take a close look at the area and do some hiking up the canyon. After we set up camp, we looked around and found some old antique glass bottles that were still in one piece, so we were pretty sure we were in the right spot, even though the old adobe stage stop building was long gone.

The next morning my son and I parked the ATV off the side of the perimeter road and hiked up the canyon. It took us a good hour of solid hiking through dry washes and cacti to get to the upper part of the canyon. We started looking for possible

RANDOM TANGENTS

locations of a vein we thought would be slightly out of vision from the old stage stop.

The first problem we ran into was that this mountainous area was capped with a limestone carbonate, and it was impossible to see vein structures through this cap. The surface was sharp and would eat up the bottom of your boots quickly; if you fell, it would tear your clothes or rip your skin. I came to find out later that the geological term for this surface was "tear-pants weathering."

We hiked for most of the day in the bowl of the canyon without finding any traces of diggings. They might have been grown over or the markings had washed away in the ninety years that had passed. The next day I had my son drop me off early so I could hike up the canyon again with my instruments to see if I could pick up any soundings. He and his grandfather had plans to ride the ATV around the lakebed and scout out the area. They were always planning and having fun wherever we went.

I made sure to carry plenty of water and a little snack as the days were getting hotter and I was going to be out by myself. I spent the day trying to sound everywhere I thought there could possibly be a vein structure but didn't have any luck. I quickly realized this wasn't going to be easy. I hiked back to camp late in the afternoon and joined my father and son for an evening cookout and some quiet time under the stars. It was magical. During the night, the temperature dropped considerably, and you needed a good sleeping bag or a couple of blankets for covers.

The next day we saw some cowboys down at the corral with several cattle. I don't know how a cow would survive out here in the desert. The cows always knew where the water was, though,

THE LOST IVANPAH SILVER VEIN

and late in the evening they would appear out of nowhere to find the nearest watering trough or hole. I asked the cowboys if they had ever seen any mining operations up in the canyon. They said they never came across anything up in that canyon, but they were always on horseback chasing cattle and not looking for anything like a prospect hole.

Over the next four years I came back several times to walk up the canyon to see if I could find anything. It was a good excuse to camp out and get a good hike in, but I was still serious about finding the vein.

On one trip I brought along my dowser friend, Dave, to see if he could have any luck. As we were about halfway across the dry lakebed, Dave told me to stop. He pulled out his dowsing rods with some silver taped to the ends and started turning in a circle. He pulled right to the canyon we were going to be walking up even though I hadn't pointed it out yet! This was promising.

We parked alongside the perimeter road so we could hike up from there. Dave didn't move all that fast as he was getting older and had diabetes. We hiked for a little over an hour and got to a spot that was just around a bend of a protrusion of the mountain that stuck out into the canyon. Dave pulled out his dowsing rods again. The rods pulled just around the bend. Dave said he thought there was a silver vein right there, so we marked out where he thought it ran. It was down in a wash area next to the mountain so it wouldn't be too hard to dig. He said he had several other small draws on his rods, but most likely they were just stringer veins.

This area would match the story as you couldn't quite see where the old stage station used to be. We decided to walk around some more to see if we would come across any other areas that would warrant looking at. At the end of the day Dave said the first area had the strongest draw and that is where he would dig. That was good enough for me. Now I needed to bring up a few tools to see if I could uncover the vein.

A few months later I made the trip back and brought a pick, a shovel, and some sample bags. I hiked up early in the morning again, spent the day digging, but couldn't find any indications of earlier digging or a vein. I started doubting that this was where McGill had found the vein.

Over the next couple of years, this particular area became a wilderness study area; mining and mechanical traffic were prohibited. I couldn't understand this as there was nothing in this area. It was dry desert with a few wild burros; it wasn't anything the normal person would drive out to have a look at or hike in.

The last time I went there, I took a friend from Pueblo, Colorado, along, who was gung-ho about finding the vein. We camped in the dry lakebed and hiked up the canyon to have a good look the second day we were there. On the third day, another friend of mine, Jim—the geologist from Tucson—showed up as he was doing some mineral exploration not too far away. We all hiked up the canyon early the next morning, and Jim gave us insight on the rock formation and possible places to look. All in all, he wasn't sure we would find anything. We headed back to camp and had a few beers and cooked out that evening.

The next morning Jim suggested driving up the road going over the mountain to the east to see what we could find. We did so and came across a big mining complex that seemed to have been shut down for years. I believe this was the Ivanpah

THE LOST IVANPAH SILVER VEIN

mining district and could have been the mine in John's story. There were several mine entrances and shafts that we explored.

We had a good day just exploring and early the next morning my friend from Pueblo and I hiked up the canyon one last time. As we got up there, I decided to go up a small wash that led up the side of the mountain. I didn't think the vein would be up this high, but I wanted to make sure I covered everything 100 percent since this was our last day.

I was nearing the top when I saw a chunk of brown rock the size of a five-gallon bucket lying at the bottom of the wash. It sure looked like ore out of a vein. As I continued to climb just a little further, I found more pieces. In a few more feet, there it was, right along the side of the wash. You could see where McGill had chiseled out some pieces and there was still an old bucket and a medicine tin lying there. It had been ninety years and the desert hadn't rusted out the bucket or medicine tin! We took them with us as we headed back to camp, along with a few plastic baggies of material I chiseled out of the vein. I thought I would run an assay on them even though one could never mine in this area now. The small assay didn't show all that much, so further sampling would have to be done, but there really was no point.

Some people approve of the ban on mining minerals back in this desolate country. I know mining is looked down on by many, but think about this for a minute: Where would we get concrete if it weren't for aggregate mining? How could we build our cars, kitchen faucets, and contacts for our cell phones if it weren't for mining? Electric cars have electric motors with massive copper windings. According to one estimate, we would have to open up twenty times the number of copper mines we have now to produce enough copper to run all our vehicles on electricity! If we shut down mining everywhere, where would we be?

A scary thing happened one time when I camped out on the dry lakebed in my Ford camper van for a week. It was fall and the weather was moderately warm, so I left the side door on my van open while I slept. One night while I was asleep a dark force that I could not see pinned me to my bed; I couldn't move. My mother had once told me that if I ever encountered a dark force, just say, "What in the name of the Lord do you want?" I remembered my mother's words, and that is what I said. Suddenly the force left, and I could move again. This had never happened before and to be honest it was a little scary.

I came out here with the thought of confronting my ego about how it manipulated my everyday life. I wanted a clear picture of how it operated and influenced the choices that I make. It was a quest for knowledge of self. I hiked and walked many hours during the day while there thinking about the question of ego. The walking helped me concentrate and think. Was the dark force part of the ego? I had been out there for seven days and after this incident, I decided to call it quits and headed back to Las Vegas the next day.

Later, I mentioned my experience with the dark force to my brother Jim. He just looked at me for a minute and said that it had happened to him on three different occasions. He said he couldn't move as this dark force had him pinned to the bed, and he couldn't fight it. He said he hadn't told anyone. He didn't know why it happened, but it was disconcerting to say the least. It was something you didn't talk about openly as people would think you were a little touched.

CHAPTER NINETEEN
End of the Hunt

During the search for treasures, which lasted from 1993 until 2003, I learned many things using conventional and scientific methods, and sometimes using an occult or psychic approach in finding things—and in not finding them. Whatever could or might work, I was game to try. I have had too many unexplained experiences in life not to explore unconventional methods.

During several years, my mother accumulated stacks of old treasure hunting magazines at her used bookstore and I went through all of them looking to see if anything seemed interesting or worthwhile. Often these stories were totally fabricated with pictures and names to make you believe they were authentic. In the end, I chose three stories to investigate that seemed the most plausible. The following story will clearly show how the art of fabrication works.

The article had a picture of a depleted barn that was supposed to be close to Greeley, Colorado. The article indicated the names of the owners of the property along with the treasure story of a buried cache of gold. First, I went to the courthouse in Greeley and searched the land records and titles. They had ledgers going back into the 1800s, however I didn't find the exact names I was looking for on land ownership deeds. I decided to go and see the county sheriff. I thought if anybody

RANDOM TANGENTS

in this county knew where that barn was, he probably did. When I showed him the picture, he laughed and said that barn was nowhere in his county. He said that this whole story was a fabrication as far as he was concerned.

There were two other stories from these magazines that I chased out. To investigate one of them, I spent twelve days backpacking in a wilderness area around Chama, New Mexico, at the end of May when there was still snow in the trees. I was looking for a stash of $20 gold pieces under a rock surrounded by a circle of oak trees.

The story goes that two miners were mining back in this mountainous area and they were doing fairly well on a gold vein they were chasing back into the mountain. Each week one of the miners would go to town and trade in the gold they had for more supplies and $20 gold pieces, which equaled an ounce of gold. When the miner returned to camp with the supplies, he would supposedly split the gold evenly with his partner.

However, the miner who always stayed at the camp started noticing that after returning from town, his partner would go on a hike into the woods, so he decided to follow him one day. He watched his partner pull some gold pieces out of his pocket and then reach in his jacket and pull out a small bag with some more $20 gold pieces. He was in an area that was circled with oak trees and a rock in the center. He slid back the rock, and in a hole underneath there was a stash of $20 gold coins—a lot more than his share would have been. The miner watching his partner went back to camp and confronted him when he returned. They got into a heated argument and he shot his partner, then took off—leaving the mine and the stash of gold pieces.

END OF THE HUNT

Sometime later a sheepherder happened to stumble upon the mine and found a gold watch lying on the ground and picked it up. When he got back to town, a fellow noticed that the watch had belonged to the miner who hadn't been seen for a while, and they figured the sheepherder had killed him. The western justice system quickly hanged him as a murderer. Years later the miner who killed his partner rode into town and confessed the murder to a priest. He said the gold still lay under the stone as he didn't want any part of it. He was never seen again.

After being dropped off at the edge of the forest I used my topographical map and compass to find my way back into the most probable area where the old mine was located. I had packed enough provisions for two weeks if I rationed them. During the first five days the sun came out in the morning then it would start sleeting in the afternoon. By the sixth day, the snow was melting from under the trees. This created a lot of runoff water, so the area became muddy and boggy. Thankfully I had good hiking boots and plenty of wool socks to keep my feet dry. At night I would look for a place high up on a hillside that was dry and out of the mud to set up camp.

In a couple of days, my search was getting closer to where I thought the lost mine should have been, and the undergrowth was much heavier. It was starting to feel like finding the proverbial needle in the haystack. On my twelfth day I studied my topographical map and saw a house and a road not far from where I was. The house was surrounded by national forest on three sides. As I walked by, I struck up a conversation with the older lady who lived there. She said she rented rooms out for overnight guests, but you had to bring your own sleeping bag or blankets. She had a big kitchen you could share and a living room full of antiques and an upright red piano.

I decided to stay the night and paid her the $10. She let me use her phone and I called my father, who said he would be there the next day to pick me up. The lady went on to tell me her husband had passed away and that she and her daughter were trying to keep the place going. She was a retired schoolteacher and now she was just trying to enjoy living there. She had hummingbird feeders up around the house and I counted over thirty hummingbirds flying around. She said that people would come up here on the weekends from the city and just relax and enjoy the area. That night after a few more people showed up, she came down from upstairs with a full-length dress on and started playing the piano. It was great fun and she was happy to be entertaining us.

She knew about the story of the gold pieces and she believed that it was true. She said one time she had a group stay with her for two weeks looking for it. Even though they said they knew exactly where it was, they couldn't find it. As far as she knew, the gold coin cache was still up there somewhere!

The third story from the treasure magazines involved a rancher who came across a cache of repeating rifles while chasing some horse thieves. He had ridden his horse down the Davies Valley in California and across the border during the chase. When he was coming back, he went up a side canyon and found a cave with a cache of repeating rifles. They were still in boxes and looked like they had been there for some time. He grabbed a couple and decided to return later to get the rest. However, in the end he never took the time to go back. Were they still there? Adventure was calling. Here we go again!

END OF THE HUNT

My father, son, and I camped in Davies Valley and we brought along my father's van and ATV to do some searching. My son and I got on the ATV early one morning and went south. Within a couple of miles, we saw lots of junk cars lying around with bullet holes in them. I thought that possibly we were in Mexico by this time, but we never saw any border signs. It was deserted and desolate country, and in the far distance we saw what looked like a big industrial plant. We checked out a couple of side canyons to get a feel for the area before heading back to camp.

About fifteen minutes after we returned to camp that day, two border patrol vehicles pulled up and an officer got out to talk to us for a minute. He said that while monitoring the area they had picked up movement in the valley, so they came to investigate if there were possible immigrants coming through. We told him we had just come from there on our ATV and hadn't seen anyone and that it was likely us who set the sensors off. He didn't want to believe us, and he said they would see for themselves. As they were about to take off, the other vehicle got stuck on top of a rock. This was like a keystone cop comedy! The first guy had to get out, hook a pull rope up to the second vehicle, and pull it off the rock. By the time they got everything unhooked, the so-called intruders would have probably been in the hills hiding. We couldn't stop laughing as we watched this play out.

The next morning, I took off early as my son and father wanted to hang out. I didn't quite go as far as we had gone the day before and came across several side canyons that I searched in hope of finding the cave with the rifles. I didn't have any luck, but I did find one canyon with an oasis in the middle of it. It had some palm trees and a small spring with water—right in the middle of the desert! I kneeled down to get a drink but had to wait a minute to let the wasps move aside. As I got up, I noticed a desert fox looking over the ridge at me from above. It was probably thirsty too and was wondering what the heck I was doing there.

I climbed up the side of the canyon, which wasn't very deep, but I had to be careful as there were cholla cacti everywhere. Some people call them "jumping cactus" as they seem to catch on anything easily and don't let go. As I was climbing, I must have wondered too close to a wasp nest and the next thing I knew they were swarming me. I jumped back so I wouldn't get stung and landed in a large cholla cactus. Several of the clumps deeply embedded between my lower arm and my bicep. Luckily, that day I had a hunting knife on my belt. I cut the chollas off, leaving their thorns in my arm. Later I pulled them out one by one. My arm turned black and yellow for the next week as it healed. I despise (and respect) those cacti to this day, and I am always extremely careful around them.

When I made it back to camp that afternoon, my father was showing my son how to shoot his pistol. I wasn't into it as I don't handle loud noises that well anymore. Anyway, my son thought it was great to learn how to shoot grandpa's pistol.

We headed back to cooler country after a few days of camping out and riding the ATV around. In the end I believe that it was another fabricated story, but it was a chance to experience a different part of the country.

Adventure Awaits

If I needed to do research using old maps or find old books or publications about the southwest, I used the Denver Public

END OF THE HUNT

Library as they have a superb Western history section. Next I would go to the public library in Phoenix to see what they had in their archives. There also used to be a good mining museum in Phoenix, which had a lot of research material on old mines and history.

I traveled a lot as I worked on projects in Nevada, Arizona, and California from 1994 through 2003. For a while I had a small pickup truck and camped out a lot in the desert so that I could go searching on weekends. Later, I bought a Ford camper van so that I could have better accommodations when working in or close to a town. Most times I would work until a job was finished then take off for several months and sleep under the stars while searching for the next treasure. This is not everyone's lifestyle but being out under the stars at night was something that I came to enjoy. Looking for a treasure became the reason to get away and not the primary goal. Yes, I would do the research and spend the hours looking but it was more of a spiritual journey in the end.

Maybe the war experience had something to do with it, I don't know. Now I could enjoy the stars and the universe without being constantly focused on listening for sounds and watching for movement to survive. I could escape into a totally relaxed state as there were no threats to concern me.

One thing happened when I was working on building a pumping station in Watsonville, California, during the summer of one of those years. I had my 1976 Ford camper van all fixed up with everything I needed, so I was pretty self-contained and had bought a membership in a health club to work out and grab a shower each night. What more could one ask for being a gypsy? One night I had a dream of standing in a dry stream bed, which had some trees along the sides and behind me was a set of stairs going down into a pipe or tunnel. As I was looking up the stream bed, two tigers started running toward me. My choices were either to run, go down the steps into the intake, or pick up a branch and fight them off. I picked up the branch, and when they were closing in on me, I dropped the branch and sat down. They stopped and looked at me and then I woke up. The picture stuck in my mind!

The next day, I drove up the coast to Santa Cruz where I went into a bookstore to look for something to read. As I was going down the aisles, on one of the shelves I noticed a book with the two tigers from my dream on the cover. It was Peter Levine's *Walking the Tiger: Healing Trauma*. I bought the book!

The book is about how people get traumatized by reliving the same traumatic point in their life over and over, thus creating a dragon that they can't escape. It tells of how animals deal with traumatic moments and then go on living normally by shaking the negative energy off. I think it was meant for me to read. I needed to learn not to think about and relive certain past events in my life. I have recommended the book over the years to people who I think need to read it to help them shake off their own demons.

All the people you meet during the years, even though briefly, form the tapestry of your life, which continues to grow as time goes on. These interactions create different perspectives on how you view other people and in how they view you.

I wish you all the best in *your* treasure hunt in life—whatever it may be. Remember that the search is more about finding out about yourself and how you relate to the universe. Life is about the journey!

Until next time!

Greg Hawk

Epilogue

In 2003 my mother asked me to think seriously about my future and retirement. She saw I enjoyed adventure and told me that I should write about everything that I experienced while traveling and living out in the desert or mountains. I listened and started back working full-time building dams and water resource projects, mostly in the western U.S., in hopes I would have a few cents saved up for retirement—whatever that is. The writing of this book is the putting down on paper of some of the adventures I have experienced in life. One can never do justice using the written word to some of the things you see, feel, or experience, but I tried.

The challenge of building water projects kept me engaged and I enjoyed it, though I occasionally did get an urge to camp out again. In fact, I did go out a couple of times just to get away for a few weeks by myself and reconnect with nature and the universe by just being under the stars.

I read and learned much over the years about homeopathic medicine, spirituality, physics, Western history, religions, philosophy, psychology, and many other subjects. I continued my search for the truth of why we are here and who we are. These are deep and perplexing questions that one may never find the answers to, but the search is surely going to bring one closer to

RANDOM TANGENTS

the truth and understanding of the universe—and may help in elevating us above our everyday dramas.

I still work occasionally depending on how much time I must devote to a particular project. I still like the interaction of a group of people who get together to accomplish a goal and work as a team. It is still satisfying to see a project come together and see workers involved take pride in it. It is a good part of human evolution. If we could all work and play together instead of going to war because of someone's ego or a company's bottom line, then I think the world would become a much better place for all.

My Australian wife, Suzanne, and I still are good friends as she lives in Cairns, close to her twin sister and son. She has a granddaughter who she adores and is a big part of her life. We decided to finally get a divorce in 2005 after twenty years of marriage as we had only seen each other twice in twelve years. I went back to Australia in 2003 and 2017 to see her and friends that I still have there. The place we used to have on the waterfront in Port Douglas has been completely removed and turned into a park. The top and bottom pubs are still there but have been renovated to adapt to the massive number of tourists that now come to this once, sleepy fishing village. The main downtown street has been rebuilt with T-shirt, fast food and curio shops for tourists. The flavor of this once small village has been changed forever.

My children are both successful and have children of their own. Now I am the grandfather who gets to play with the grandkids. It is good seeing them grow up and hopefully, in time, becoming what they wish to be.

May you soar with the hawk and have the keen eyesight to see things for what they really are and to fully realize we are all

EPILOGUE

here for a limited amount of time. Make the best of each day you have as a new adventure.

Cheers,
Greg Hawk

About the Author

GREG HAWK was born in 1948 and grew up in Illinois on a small farm until going off to college and then to war. After his return, he started questioning a lot of things in life. The further down the road (rabbit hole) he went, the deeper and more profound the questions became. Sometimes the answers didn't readily appear, or they were not the answers he was expecting.

Now at seventy-one years old, he is starting another business, working on a patent, and writing a book. Retirement doesn't seem to be in his vocabulary as there is so much that he still wants to accomplish.

He has studied homeopathic medicine, physics (including superstring theory), radionics, psionics, psychology, philosophy, religion, history, and even delved into metaphysics. Throughout life, he has worked in the construction trades, been a principal of a successful construction company, the owner of a scuba diving business in Australia, and a treasure hunter.

He has faced death numerous times in war, in the water, and while climbing in the mountains during his adventures. He has always felt that there must be a force watching over him and he has something yet to accomplish before leaving Spaceship Earth.

His mother owned a little used bookstore in her later years and always wanted him to write a book about his treasure

RANDOM TANGENTS

hunting escapades, underwater encounters, and travels to exotic places.

This book is the culmination of several years reflection and documenting of a time period in his life. A memoir, an adventure, a reflection of oneself could all be descriptions of how the author looks at the world through this book.

www.ingramcontent.com/pod-product-compliance
Lightning Source LLC
Chambersburg PA
CBHW071340080526
44587CB00017B/2901